IMAGES
of America

JENKINTOWN

Jenkintown, Pa.

Old York Road runs through the center of Jenkintown. The bank building designed by local architect Horace Trumbauer, one of the more notable structures along the commercial corridor, stands at the northeast corner of West Avenue and Old York Road. Farther north, the Strawbridge & Clothier department store marks the northern edge of the borough. The southern end of town faces the expanse of the Old York Road Country Club, land owned since 1697 by the John Barnes Trust of Abington Friends Meeting and School. (Courtesy of Old York Road Historical Society.)

ON THE COVER: In 1910, the family of Rosa M. Towne (1827–1909) erected a fountain in her memory owing to her great love of horses. Towne was a local artist best known for illustrating the wildflowers mentioned in Shakespeare's plays. The fountain was placed under the care of the Montgomery County Branch of the Women's Pennsylvania Society for the Prevention of Cruelty to Animals, then based in Jenkintown. The Jenkintown Improvement Association added an illuminated sign behind the fountain in early 1916. (Courtesy of Old York Road Historical Society.)

IMAGES
of America

JENKINTOWN

Marion K. Rosenbaum and
the Old York Road Historical Society

ARCADIA
PUBLISHING

Copyright © 2024 by Marion K. Rosenbaum and the Old York Road Historical Society
ISBN 978-1-4671-6128-2

Published by Arcadia Publishing
Charleston, South Carolina

Printed in the United States of America

Library of Congress Control Number: 2023952473

For all general information, please contact Arcadia Publishing:
Telephone 843-853-2070
Fax 843-853-0044
E-mail sales@arcadiapublishing.com

Visit us on the Internet at www.arcadiapublishing.com

On February 8, 1907, following a snowstorm, the Jenkinstown Lyceum building (today's Jenkintown Library) stands as one of the few structures at the northern end of town. The trolley competed with horse-drawn wagons and sleighs in the days before the automobile became a common sight. At the time, the northern suburbs of Philadelphia were rural, with small villages breaking up the expanse of farms. Of the small villages dotting the landscape along and adjacent to the Old York Road, Jenkintown was the largest by far. (Courtesy of Old York Road Historical Society.)

CONTENTS

ACKNOWLEDGMENTS

In preparation for the celebration of Jenkintown's 150th anniversary as an independent borough and school district, Marion K. Rosenbaum consulted with Jill Takacs, Jenkintown School District's superintendent, and David Ballard and Deborra Sines Pancoe of the borough council about doing a photographic history book of the community. With enthusiastic encouragement, Marion set off to complete this book, enlisting the resources and collections of the Old York Road Historical Society as a partner in the endeavor. All photographs contained herein are from the collections of the society unless otherwise noted.

Many people have generously lent guidance, stories, photographs, and help along the way, including Andrew Barnett, the Reverend Luke Billman, Ben Bergman (Jenkintown 150th anniversary chair), Rafael Campo, the late Shirley Curry, Bill and Penny Cutler, Glenn DePretis, Andrew Edelman, Jon Edelman, Michael Foy, Leo Greenberry, Charlene Jefferson, Abbie Johnson, Wendy Klinghoffer, George Locke (borough manager), Ellen Herr, Barbara Jacobs, David Lembeck, Robert MacFarland, Nina Meister (Jenkintown Library director), Penny and Lou Riggs, Anastasia Rousseau (Arcadia University archivist), Tom Scott (chief of police), Steve Spindler, Maureen Stephenson, John Still, Stuart Tollen, Tom Tompkins, and Chuck Whitney.

In addition, Old York Road Historical Society members who ably assisted were Eileen Koolpe, Ed Landau, Daniel Myers, James Rubillo, Stephanie Walsh, and Tom Wieckoswki. Going above and beyond the call of duty were Susan Adler, who brought her editorial skills to bear throughout the project, and Leslie Bell who scanned and organized virtually all the images for this book. Finally, as Marion and I have gone through the photographs and files of the society, I have been made keenly aware of the tremendous work former society archivist Joyce Root did over many years in organizing and cataloging the photographic collections of the society. It is a testament to which we will be forever indebted.

With the great care and dedication that both Marion and I have put into this book, it is our hope that *Jenkintown* will prove useful and edifying to the citizens of this community both now and well into the future. Happy anniversary and enjoy!

—David B. Rowland, president
Old York Road Historical Society

INTRODUCTION

The inspiration for this book was to create a history for the 150th anniversary of the founding of Jenkintown's borough and schools in 1874. But the scope of the book soon broadened to include the beginnings of "Jenkins Town" from the time of William Penn, his dealings with Native Americans, and the early families who settled in our area.

It is difficult to document much about the Unami, or turtle clan, of the Lenni Lenape, or Delawares, who called eastern Pennsylvania their home. There is no authentic image of Chief Tamanend, who probably was the Indian who negotiated with Penn, as he was chief of chiefs at that time. Ongoing archeological and genetic research will no doubt add to future understanding. More documentation is to be found of early immigrants to our area from various European lands: John Barnes from England, William Jenkins from Wales, and others who came mostly from Ireland, Scotland, and Germany. Most were fleeing from the civil wars in England and Germany and oppression from taxation by both church and state. It is not by accident that many religious institutions were organized first by Quakers and then by Episcopalians, Presbyterians, Catholics, Methodists, and Baptists.

Immigrants William Jenkins and his son Stephen are credited with the naming of Jenkins Town, where their extended family settled and became active in developing the area. Later families who came were the Cottmans, Ridpaths, Mathers, Johnsons, Leedoms, Shoemakers, Wanamakers, and Newbolds. They became residents, opened businesses, and were memorialized with street names. Other family street names were changed—Spaeter Road became Highland Avenue, and Beechwood Avenue (named for the residence of William C. Kent) became West Avenue. More streets show the diversity of trees planted by early settlers: maple, walnut, willow, cherry, cedar, and elm. More names came from the old country: York, Vernon, and Runnymede. Some names reflect geography: Highland, Summit, East (became Greenwood), and West. And some street names are unexplainable without further research.

Until 1820, Philadelphia was the largest city in the country. The surrounding regions were agricultural. Early inns and taverns and those businesses that catered to the carriage trade and their horses thrived throughout the 19th century. The Jenkinstown Lyceum, started in 1838 by Mary Jenkins Ross, was an important cultural center for learning and served as a catalyst by nurturing many organizations documented in this history—churches, schools, and other cultural, civic, and social organizations—that make our community unique. The coming of the railroad in 1855 initiated a steady migration from the city to the country and the evolution of what we now know as suburban. As streets were laid out and more houses built, shops opened for dry goods, coal, lumber, and much more.

The residents who pushed for a separate borough in 1874 were motivated by taxes—taxes going to a large rural township that was not focused on developing the infrastructure (sidewalks, good roads, etc.) of the small commercial hub. The original petition for establishing the borough had included farmland, but the court rejected this, allowing only the quickly developing village to separate. And so Jenkintown was born. Once self-governing was established with a burgess (now mayor) and borough council, projects proceeded quickly regarding roads, paving, utilities, police enforcement, and fire protection. Starting in 1922 to 1931, six land annexations were negotiated with Abington Township, which added small areas to the borough, but usually after hard negotiations and reciprocal considerations were arranged.

Because our schools were small compared to neighboring regional districts, Jenkintown maintained an optimal learning environment. Past residents have been willing to increase taxes for more land, new buildings, and new additions to school property in order not to be consolidated into larger school districts. Fortunately for Jenkintown, teachers had careers and not just jobs. Many principals and superintendents moved into the community, stayed here, and sent their children and grandchildren to Jenkintown schools. The many traditions unique to Jenkintown became ties that bind. Color Day, in particular, has become an important event each year, eagerly anticipated by young and old alike.

Changes in transportation brought more people to the area to settle or find rest and relaxation. More commercial buildings created a town center, and Jenkintown became more self-sufficient with its own newspaper, banks, food stores, and doctors. Businesses flourished that focused on the building trades with carpentry, welding, and bricklaying. After the coming of the railroad and the Beechwood Inn, automobiles, trolleys, buses, and air travel eventually replaced bicycles, horses, and carriages. Communication evolved with the coming of the telephone, radio, and television and more recently with satellite, cell towers, smartphones, computers, the internet, and websites. Not all of this growth is covered in this history, but it gives a hint of times to come.

The commercial pictures of buildings and businesses that no longer exist should bring back many memories. The oldest photographs, taken by William T. Bitting, capture the late 1890s. Many later images starting in the late 1920s are by Jenkintown school graduate, local resident, and *Times-Chronicle* photographer Harry Utzy. The chapter is a virtual walk up and down the streets of Jenkintown and shows then and now locations.

Wars since the beginning of our country have impacted our local town and quality of life, starting with the American Revolution, the Civil War and abolition of slavery, two world wars, Korea, Vietnam, Desert Storm, Desert Shield, and Afghanistan. Various veterans' organizations help us remember, by holding regular parades and memorializing those who have died. Police, fire, school bands, and other patriotic organizations are also an integral part of our many holiday celebrations.

Civic and social groups that are active now but not in this book are the Breathing Room (providing cancer support services) and Second Chances thrift shop (providing funds for domestic violence prevention). Other groups are no longer within the borough but are part of our history. The Jenkintown Day Nursery and the Old York Road Historical Society are now based in Abington. The Settlement Music School, which was formerly the Jenkintown branch, is now in Willow Grove. The Eastern Montgomery Chamber of Commerce, now located in Fort Washington, was formerly the Jenkintown Chamber of Commerce. Important organizations that have not survived but contributed greatly to Jenkintown's past are the Lions Club, the Independent Order of Odd Fellows, the Moose Lodge, and the Jenkintown Women's Club.

Many stories of the past keep circling back to the Jenkinstown Lyceum building. So many of our organizations started in this building or had a temporary home in this structure as they grew, including all but one of Jenkintown's churches. This building is now the home of the Jenkintown Library, founded as the Abington Library Society in 1803. The library has had many dedicated librarians in its long history and continues to be an ongoing reminder that there is always more to learn if we only take the time. My hope is that this book of images will trigger more questions and that you will explore more topics that have not been covered here.

–Marion K. Rosenbaum

One

THE EARLY YEARS

In 1682, under a large elm tree at Shakamaxon, William Penn was given a wampum belt (depicting a Native American and Penn) by a group of Lenni Lenape chiefs and their wives, who created the belt from clam and whelk shell beads and leather. In return, Penn agreed to a list of items (clothing, pipes, tobacco, knives, blankets, etc.) that were distributed among the tribes present. Tamanend (c. 1675–c. 1701), chief of chiefs at that time, most likely led the Lenape delegation. His headquarters was known to overlook the Neshaminy Creek near Newtown.

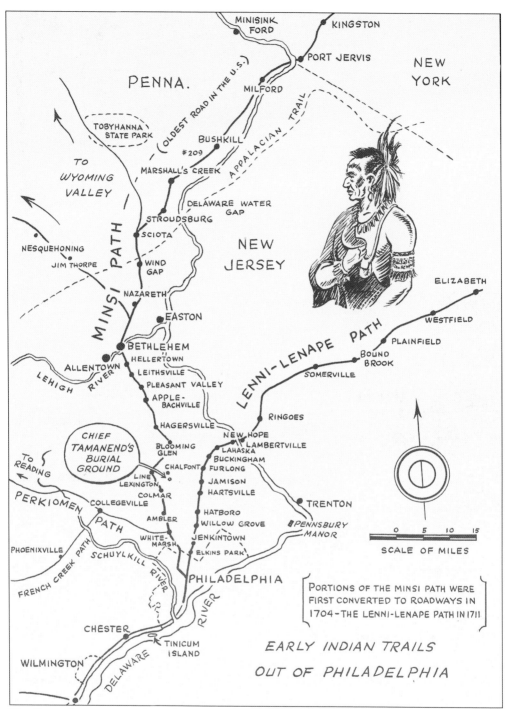

MINISINK
FORD

KINGSTON

PORT JERVIS

NEW
YORK

PENNA.

MILFORD

OLDEST ROAD IN THE U.S.

#209

TOBYHANNA
STATE PARK

BUSHKILL

MARSHALL'S CREEK

APPALACIAN TRAIL

TO
WYOMING
VALLEY

DELAWARE WATER
GAP

STROUDSBURG

SCIOTA

NEW
JERSEY

NESQUEHONING

JIM THORPE

WIND
GAP

MINSI PATH

NAZARETH

ELIZABETH

EASTON

WESTFIELD

BETHLEHEM

HELLERTOWN

LENNI-LENAPE PATH

PLAINFIELD

BOUND
BROOK

ALLENTOWN

LEITHSVILLE

LEHIGH RIVER

PLEASANT VALLEY

SOMERVILLE

APPLE-
BACHVILLE

HAGERSVILLE

RINGOES

CHIEF
TAMANEND'S
BURIAL
GROUND

NEW HOPE

BLOOMING
GLEN

LAMBERTVILLE

LAHASKA

TO
READING

CHALFONT

BUCKINGHAM
FURLONG

LINE
LEXINGTON

JAMISON

COLMAR

HARTSVILLE

PERKIOMEN

COLLEGEVILLE

TRENTON

AMBLER

HATBORO

WILLOW GROVE

PATH

PENNSBURY
MANOR

PHOENIXVILLE

FRENCH CREEK PATH

WHITE-
MARSH

JENKINTOWN

SCHUYLKILL RIVER

ELKINS PARK

0   5   10   15

SCALE OF MILES

PHILADELPHIA

FRENCH CREEK PATH

CHESTER

TINICUM
ISLAND

PORTIONS OF THE MINSI PATH WERE
FIRST CONVERTED TO ROADWAYS IN
1704 - THE LENNI-LENAPE PATH IN 1711

WILMINGTON

DELAWARE RIVER

EARLY INDIAN TRAILS
OUT OF PHILADELPHIA

The Lenni Lenape were the indigenous tribe prevalent in eastern Pennsylvania at the time of
William Penn's arrival. They had major trails that ran through their lands, including a path
between what would become Philadelphia and New York City. This trail, which cuts through
Jenkintown, was the forerunner of Old York Road. Today, the road is known as York Road as it
passes through the borough and State Route 611.

In 1803, the Cheltenham & Willow Grove Turnpike Company was chartered, and Old York Road was turned over to private ownership. This was done to improve the maintenance of the roadway at a time when there were virtually no public services. Following a survey, mile markers were placed along the route. The mile marker that still stands on the front lawn of the Jenkintown Library reads, "7 to RS, 9 to P," indicating seven miles to Rising Sun and nine miles to Philadelphia at Fourth and Vine Streets, where the road had its beginning.

The turnpike company charged for the use of the road, and tollhouses were erected along the route to collect tolls. The Jenkintown toll gate was at the southeast corner of Old York Road and Washington Lane, the southern boundary of Jenkintown. The turnpike company was purchased in the early 1890s by the People's Traction Company, and on January 19, 1895, the first trolley ran to Jenkintown. The home on the right still stands on Washington Lane. The state bought out the traction company in 1918, thus "freeing" Old York Road.

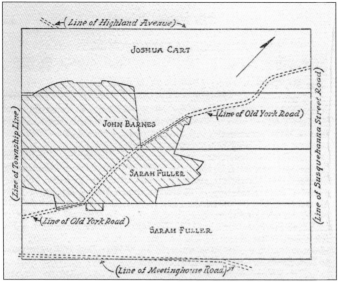

The land from which Jenkintown emerged was originally purchased from William Penn in 1683–1684 by three Quaker settlers, Joshua Cart, John Barnes, and Sarah Fuller. The two strips of land owned by Sarah Fuller were later sold to John Barnes, giving him 850 acres. When the village of Jenkintown petitioned for independent status from Abington Township in 1874, the court only permitted developed land to be included; any farmland was specifically excluded.

In 1697, Barnes deeded 120 acres to be used for the founding of a Quaker school (Abington Friends School) and the erection of a Quaker meetinghouse. George Boone, uncle to Daniel Boone, was an early teacher from 1716 to 1720. The school has continuously operated on this same ground since its founding and is considered one of the oldest schools in Pennsylvania. From 1931 to 1966, the school was all female but otherwise has provided coeducational education from kindergarten through 12th grade.

In 1683, Abington meeting had its beginnings in the home of Richard Wall in present-day Elkins Park. The meeting moved into a meetinghouse constructed on the land given by John Barnes around 1702. The building was expanded in 1786 and again in 1797 into what are its present dimensions. The building of the meetinghouse in 1702 was quite important in the history of the settlement of Jenkintown. The meeting attracted folks from all over the area. Located between the mills on the Pennypack and Tacony Creeks, the meeting had a number of families to draw upon. They came via Meetinghouse Road. Other roads led to the meeting, including the Jenkintown, Fox Chase, and Abington (now Washington Lane) roads, further connecting the surrounding communities with the meeting. The Barnes gift of land, then, was transformative to the entire area. Interestingly, the Barnes Trust still owns the grounds of the school and meetinghouse in addition to the grounds of the Abington Club. (Abington Friends Meeting.)

The oldest section of this house was built by Stephen Jenkins (1680–1761), who is credited with the founding of Jenkins Town. He came with his parents, William (1648–1712) and Elizabeth Griffith Jenkins, and several siblings from Tenby, Pembrokeshire, Wales, in 1685. He moved to Abington in 1697 and purchased 400 acres from John Barnes. The home was later owned by two generations of the Schofield family before being sold in 1850 to William H. Newbold and named Vernon. The house still stands overlooking Washington Lane.

Stephen Jenkins built an inn and tavern on the east side of Old York Road at West Avenue around 1725. His son Phineas Jenkins (1701–1791) and his wife, Sarah, managed the inn and tavern. After Phineas died, the inn was called Widow Jenkins Tavern until the Cottman family took it over in 1837. This was a prominent and important stop on the stagecoach route between Philadelphia and New York City. The inn was demolished when West Avenue was cut through.

Jesse Jenkins (a grandson of Stephen Jenkins), born in 1749, and his wife, Mary, lived on the west side of Old York Road. Because Mary was not a Quaker, Jesse was disowned by the meeting after refusing to acknowledge his error. Their daughter Mary Jenkins was born and grew up in this home. A group of doctors later operated out of this location: Drs. Betts, Paxson, Tyson, and Walton, followed by Dr. Shoemaker.

Mary Jenkins Ross (1775–1845) was married in the Philadelphia Monthly Meeting to John Ross in 1795. He was a lawyer, Pennsylvania state representative, US representative, district judge, and Pennsylvania Supreme Court judge. The couple lived in Easton until Judge Ross died in 1834. Mary then moved back to Jenkintown and lived on the east side of Old York Road with several of her children. She donated the land and constructed the Jenkinstown Lyceum building. Her home was demolished in 1938.

The Jenkinstown Lyceum was founded in 1838 as a cultural, educational, and social organization. By 1840, there were 188 members who met weekly on Thursday evenings. Dues were 50¢ annually. Discussions, lectures, debates, and the free interchange of sentiments were encouraged. The group was active for many years but never fully recovered from divisions over the issue of abolition in the 1850s. While the organization rarely met after the Civil War, the building was rented out to various groups. It gradually fell into disrepair until it was purchased in 1909 by the Abington Library Society.

In 1867, a Masonic lodge was formed in Jenkintown, Friendship Lodge No. 400. For the first six years, it met in a wood-framed building on the third floor at 311 Old York Road. In 1870, the lodge took steps to construct its own building, and in 1873, it moved into Masonic Hall. The large building had spaces that were rented to other organizations and businesses. The north door carries a sign for the Abington Library. The Abington Library Society was founded in 1803 as a private shareholder library. The collection moved with the librarian until it was settled into Masonic Hall in 1878.

William C. Kent, a mill owner, purchased 103 acres in 1854 and built a home called Beechwood overlooking the present-day Jenkintown train station. Kent is credited with having started the cotton futures market. In 1855, the North Pennsylvania Railroad Company put down a train line passing through Kent's property and terminating at Gwynedd. R.J. Dobbins, a later owner of Beechwood, converted the house with a large addition into an inn and marketed the Beechwood Hotel as a tourist destination beginning in 1877.

The Kent landholdings extended over Tookany Creek into present-day Wyncote. The creek is part of the Tookany-Tacony Frankford Watershed. In the Juniata section of Philadelphia, the Tookany-Tacony Creek joins the Jenkintown Creek, whose headwaters are on the Abington Friends Meeting land, to become the Frankford Creek, which flows into the Delaware River.

When Greenwood Avenue was laid down around 1858, a petition for a train stop was approved in 1859 under the name of Cheltenham. The wooden platform was replaced with a station in 1862, and the station was renamed Jenkintown. In 1869, double tracks were installed, and in 1872, a more substantial station of stone was erected. An elevated pedestrian walkway was erected that connected the station to the Beechwood Hotel.

In 1931, when the rail lines were converted to electric power, architect Horace Trumbauer designed a new station in the Tudor Revival style. For a time, the station was leased to several restaurants: Greenwood Grille (1986–1990), Stazi Milano (1991–2001), Station Grille (2003–2004), and Jonathan's American Grille (2005–2008). When trains still ran through Jenkintown to New York City or connected to Wilkes Barre, Scranton, Buffalo, or Chicago, the station saw some 183 trains stop every weekday each way. Today, 70 trains stop each way at Jenkintown coming from or going to Glenside, Warminster, Doylestown, and West Trenton. It is still considered one of the best-served suburban train stations in the country.

Two

BOROUGH AND NATION

Jenkintown Borough purchased the former Jenkintown Methodist Episcopal Church building in 1901 for a new borough hall. Located at the southwest corner of West Avenue and Leedom Street, the building was originally a public school for Abington Township prior to becoming a church. Over the years, as the demands for public services led to bigger budgets and more personnel, the local government outgrew the building.

The borough council meeting on October 24, 1947, was a crowded affair as many of the local businessmen were out to protest a new traffic ordinance prohibiting left-hand turns on Old York Road. It also stands as a study in contrast with contemporary meetings in many aspects. Council was all male, all white, all Republican, all Christian, and everyone, including the public, dressed in business attire for the evening meetings. The burgess (mayor) at the time was Harry Fritsch Jr. He had been inducted the year before and went on to serve for 29 years.

January 1976 witnessed a new borough council taking office, this being the first time the majority of members were from the Democratic Party. From left to right are (first row) Henry Molt (R); Mary Jane Reilly (D); David Jordan, president (D); Ken McKinney, vice president (D); Gail West (D); and Henry Kuller (D); (second row) Bill DelGesso (D); Ted Kellem (D); Norval Copple (R); Ted Jensen, mayor (R); Frank Rehnert (R); Jack Plunkett (D); and Art Frantz (R).

Having long outgrown the borough hall on West Avenue, the borough purchased a property on Summit Avenue in 1978, and a new borough hall was completed in 1981. The building houses both the borough manager with the municipal staff as well as the police department. The old building was demolished in November 1981 and sold to Immaculate Conception Church. It is now a preschool play area.

The 2023 borough council is composed of all Democrats, as is the mayor. Women constitute a majority of council members, an historical first. From left to right are (first row) David Ballard, Jay Connors (president), Christian Soltysiak, and Deborra Sines Pancoe; (second row) Maxine Marlowe, Alex Bartlett, Aliza Narva, Anne MacHaffie, Alexandria Khalil, Joanne Bruno, and Gabriel Lerman (mayor). (Jenkintown Borough.)

21

Before 1890, Jenkintown only had a constable to keep the peace. Thomas York was hired that year to levy fines on men and boys who had been seen playing baseball near the railroad station on a Sunday. After World War I, a second position was created. The first police headquarters was at the rear of the borough hall. For special events, including the Fourth of July parade in 1938, the police force turned out mounted on horseback, the horses having been lent by private citizens.

By 1950, the police force had grown dramatically. Mayor Fritsch, on the right, is performing the oath of office. From left to right are (first row) Frank Sweeny, John Plunkett, Steve Malone, Jim Bustard, John McAller, and Ray Walsh; (second row) Jack Angeny, Joe Disher, Carl Butzloff, Lou Murray, Tom Huhn, and Lud McIntire. The police department reports to the mayor, unlike all other municipal services that report to the borough council through the borough manager. (Jenkintown Police Department.)

Robert J. Furlong (1929–2018) was born in Philadelphia and raised in Jenkintown. He graduated from Jenkintown High School in 1948, married his next-door neighbor, and they raised five children. After service in Korea, he joined the police force in 1957, first as a patrolman and juvenile officer, then rising to sergeant, captain (at the time of this photograph in 1984), and chief by 1990. He was also a member of the Jenkintown Lions Club and a lifetime member of the Pioneer Fire Company. He retired in 1998 after 41 years of service.

Today, Jenkintown's police force provides round-the-clock coverage for all of the borough, a vast change since the first part-time constable walked his beat in the late 1800s. Among the members of the force in 2022 are, from left to right, (first row) Frank Jaworski, Mark Welsh, Chris Kelly, Richard Tucker, David Sangree, and Anthony Matteo; (second row) Edward Culbreath, Edward Titterton, Chief Thomas Scott, Albert Sulpizio, Cory Murtagh, and Rory Tuggy. (Jenkintown Borough.)

In 1884, the Pioneer Fire Company No. 1 was formed with Hugh H. O'Neill (president), Joseph W. Hunter (vice president), Byron McCracken (secretary), Howard Fleck (financial secretary), and Thomas B. Harper (treasurer). Directors included J.W. Ridpath, George Fleck, Howard Fleck, Joseph W. Hunter, Frederick Palmer, and W.H. Thomas. After being located in several places, the company secured the southeast corner of Greenwood Avenue and Leedom Street in 1899 and moved its building to the site. However, in 1906, that building was razed, and a new station was constructed. It is still in use but has been remodeled several times.

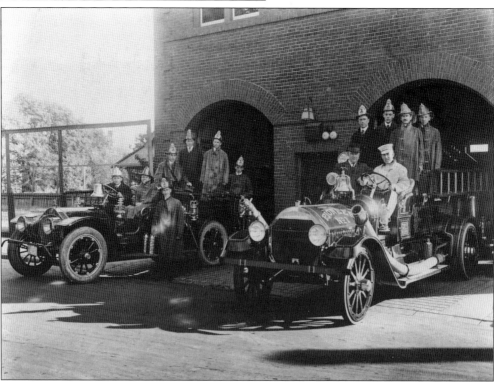

In 1909, Pioneer had an Acme hose and chemical wagon (left), with driver Otis Mather and John Williams seated next to him. The others in back are, from left to right, Cyril O'Neil, John O'Donnell, Jack King, and Richard Devlin. The man standing beside the wagon is unidentified. A Waterous pumper is on the right, with Chief Andy Graham at the wheel and the truck salesman next to him. Behind them from left to right are Barney Devlin, Carroll Griffiths, George Gock, and Harry Poole.

In 1909, Pioneer was instrumental in the organization of the Volunteer Firemen's Association of Montgomery County. The purpose was not only to improve fire service throughout the area but also to provide social opportunities for its member companies. The organization is still active. The firemen of Pioneer pose with their 1940 Seagraves pumper (left) and a 1950 Maxim pumper (right).

In 1984, the Pioneer Fire Company celebrated its 100th anniversary. The officers are, from left to right, (first row) Joseph Connolly (lieutenant), Gary Hutnick (second assistant chief), Gary Bachman (chief), Daniel Bell (chief engineer), and Michael Reifsnyder (captain); (second row) Nick Pettinati (assistant engineer).

A charter for a second volunteer company in Jenkintown was granted in 1889 to the Independent Fire Company No. 2. A one-story firehouse on rented ground was built at 609 Greenwood Avenue to hold a hand-drawn ladder truck. The company had 110 feet of hose, 30 leather buckets, axes, ladders, picks, and lanterns. The first president was Albert Weaks. From left to right are (on the ground) Howard Clayton, J.H. Hay, Bill Geris, Charles Myers (foreman), Joe Biddle, Harry Swank, Bill Burskirk, Charles McCool, and Harry Ogden; (on the truck) Dan Geary, Tom Branin, John McCool, Sam Aiman, Jeff Donnell, and Leon Hay.

The Independent Fire Company not only fought fires but had a band that marched in parades. The band members had uniforms and traveled around the area to represent Jenkintown in various ceremonies. All of the companies in the Montgomery County Firemen's Association paraded in each other's towns, and Independent had gone as far as a parade in Bethlehem in 1898.

By 1898, the 609 Greenwood Avenue lot was purchased, and two years later, a two-and-a-half-story brick building with a meeting room on the second floor was completed. In 1911, Independent Fire Company had the only motor-driven truck, a converted Columbia automobile, and the first motorized ladder apparatus.

On June 7, 1952, Independent held a parade followed by a housing ceremony for its new ladder truck. Over 20 fire companies sent representatives to the festivities. An Atlantic gas pump specifically for the fire station is on the left, and the Atlantic sign is on the right of the building. In November 2023, Jenkintown's two fire companies merged into one but will maintain both locations.

Following the return of troops after the end of World War I, Jenkintown organized a "Welcome Home Celebration" on November 8, 1919, including a grand parade and a ceremony that included a keynote speech by Samuel High, Esq. Receiving special honors was Jenkintown native Navy captain John Fred Carlton, commander of the USS *Silver Shell*, who was credited with the first American sinking of a German U-boat.

After the "Welcome Home Celebration" ceremony on the athletic field, the parade reformed and marched to the borough hall where a monument honoring those from Jenkintown who served in World War I was unveiled. The bronze plaque contains over 200 names. At the end of the day, a banquet was held under a tent erected on Greenwood Avenue, next to the Pioneer Fire Company, followed by a band concert and street dancing.

During World War II, the Jenkintown train station did duty as a departure point for recruits from throughout the area going off to service. As in World War I, many Jenkintown men and women served in the war. Jenkintown's first war casualty was James J. Gleason, who died in the Japanese attack on Pearl Harbor on December 7, 1941.

Throughout World War II, an honor roll was maintained on the front lawn of the borough hall. The list of all those who served was quite extensive. Following the war, an effort was made to honor all those who had served, but despite plans being drawn up, the monument never materialized.

The McKeown-Zane Post No. 1711 of the Veterans of Foreign Wars (VFW) was organized in July 1929 in McKinley and moved to Jenkintown in 1935, where it occupied the second floor of 805 Greenwood Avenue. In 1939, the organization purchased property on Summit Avenue. Continued growth, especially following World War II, led to the need for still larger quarters.

In 1946, the VFW purchased the Odd Fellow's Hall building as its new headquarters. Constructed in 1921, the hall was built for the Peace and Love Lodge, No. 337 of the Independent Order of Odd Fellows, a fraternal organization. The building is located on Leedom Street at Summit Avenue. A parade on November 9, 1946, marked the formal opening of the post's new home.

Following the parade, a gala dinner attended by some 300 guests was held inside the VFW hall. The hall still serves as host to community events, including a luncheon held on Memorial Day following the town's ceremonies.

The VFW post continues to mark Memorial Day and Veterans Day annually with a parade and ceremony held at the World War I monument adjacent to the borough hall. Members of the post are assisted by the post's Ladies Auxiliary, which was organized on July 24, 1937. Jenkintown veterans marching on November 11, 1999, include Bob Grooms, Andrew Pachuta, John R. Donahoe, and John Tierney.

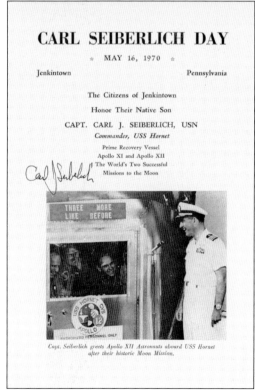

CARL SEIBERLICH DAY

☆ MAY 16, 1970 ☆

Jenkintown   Pennsylvania

The Citizens of Jenkintown
Honor Their Native Son

CAPT. CARL J. SEIBERLICH, USN
Commander, USS Hornet

Prime Recovery Vessel
Apollo XI and Apollo XII
The World's Two Successful
Missions to the Moon

Capt. Seiberlich greets Apollo XII Astronauts aboard USS Hornet after their historic Moon Mission.

The Coates-Jordan American Legion Post No. 163 was formed in 1919. It was named after two local men, George B. Coates and Paul Jordan, who were killed in the war. The post met in the Service Center Building until 1952 when the organization purchased its own structure at 403 Maple Street. During a May 1964 meeting, the post held a surprise 85th birthday party for its beloved chaplain, Rev. Alfred M. Smith, DD, a World War I veteran, shown standing center.

One of Jenkintown's most famous sons in modern times and a member of the Coates-Jordan American Legion Post was Rear Adm. Carl J. Seiberlich (1921–2006). He attended school at Immaculate Conception and graduated from Jenkintown High School in 1938. He served in the Merchant Marine before active duty in the Navy during World War II. In 1952, he received the Harmon International Aviation Trophy from President Truman, and in 1969, he assumed command of the USS *Hornet*, tasked with the recovery of the Apollo XI and XII astronauts. On May 16, 1970, his hometown celebrated him with a full day of events.

Jim Dearden passes out voting literature for the primary elections in the spring of 1982 to Louise Eccarius and Maryann Gallagher in front of the American Legion Post building on Maple Street. For many years, the post held an annual pork roast and sauerkraut dinner that attracted large numbers of folks. In 1983, the post sold its building and, due to lack of membership, folded in 2014.

Independence Day parades have been a long-standing tradition in Jenkintown. On July 4, 1914, the annual parade marched south on Old York Road, as the parades would continue to do until the 1970s. Thereafter, parades wind their way through some of the residential side streets. Following the band is the Independent Fire Company.

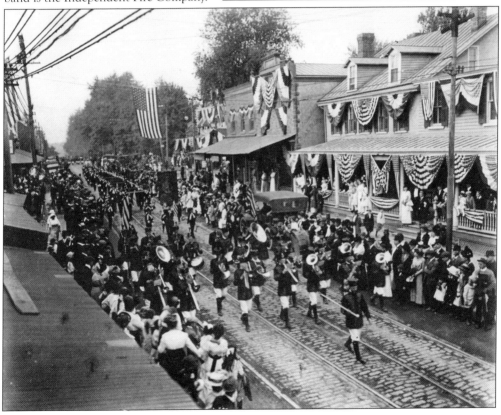

One of the earliest post offices was in the Cottman Inn on Old York Road at West Avenue. It later moved into the Service Center Building at the southwest corner of Greenwood Avenue and Old York Road and, in 1927, took up residence on Johnson Street next to the Times-Chronicle Building. Bernard A. Devlin was the postmaster beginning in 1933, and he oversaw the post office's move to its current location in 1940.

The post office relocated to the corner of West Avenue and Cedar Street where the previous public school had stood. In 1942, a mural was installed in the post office, painted by Herschel Levit (1912–1986) and entitled *George Washington's Troops on Old York Road* (location unknown). In 1955, the post office expanded its building to the east, after which time Jenkintown became a major distribution center. In 1963, the Jenkintown zip code of 19046 was established encompassing a much larger geographical area than just the borough. This explains why actor Bradley Cooper is said to have come from Jenkintown while his home was in Abington Township. (National Archives.)

For many years, the borough considered various plans for the corner parcels at Leedom Street and Greenwood Avenue. Design plans by landscape architect Ed Landau were approved in 1999 and a gazebo was designed by architect Judy Hendrixon, who coordinated the project as a member of the planning commission. Mayor Michael O'Neill dedicated the square on June 3, 2003. The project received the Planning Merit Award for improving the quality of life from the Montgomery County Planning Commission. (Ed Landau.)

Jenkintown Town Square is now considered the center of town. It replaced a number of older commercial buildings that had seen better days. Active businesses along Old York Road and West Avenue reconfigured their entrances on the street to provide easier access to the parking in the back. Many families provided funding by purchasing blocks with their names. Live music is held during the summer months, and a weekly farmers' market showcases local food and artisans.

Wilmot E. Fleming (1916–1978) was a graduate of Cheltenham High School and the University of Pennsylvania. He served on the Jenkintown School Board as president from 1954 to 1961 and was instrumental in preventing Jenkintown schools from being consolidated into a larger regional school system. He served as a Pennsylvania state representative for one year. In 1964, he became a Pennsylvania state senator, serving until his death. He was a Jenkintown Rotary Club member for 29 years and a long-standing elder and trustee at Grace Presbyterian Church.

On August 3, 2016, a celebration was held to name the Greenwood Avenue bridge the "Honorable Lawrence H. Curry Bridge." Leslie Richards (secretary of the Pennsylvania Department of Transportation), Madeleine Dean (US congresswoman), and Joe Hoeffel (former US congressman) attended. Art Haywood (Pennsylvania state senator) and Steve McCarter (Pennsylvania state representative) were also in the group. Valerie Arkoosh (Montgomery County commissioner) was present along with other county row officers: Noah Marlier (prothonotary), Sean Kilkenny (sheriff), and Bruce Hanes (register of wills). (Glenn DePretis.)

Three

SCHOOLS

When the first public school building in Jenkintown was sold to the Methodist Church in 1867, the Abington Public Schools constructed a new structure at the corner of West Avenue and Cedar Street. After the borough was formed, a new Jenkintown School District was established and the school property was transferred. In 1875, Enos Rosenberger (at the foot of steps) was principal, Mattie Rosenberger and Archanna Prince (at the window) were teachers, and George Kohl (on the right) was a school director. Other directors were George McCool, George Fleck, George Nice, Edward Everett, and Francis Triol. The first graduation certificates (for eighth grade) were issued in 1887 to Walter Fleck, John Wakeley, and Lucy Fitz.

The 1867 school building was enlarged in 1889, and in 1904, a three-story brick structure was attached to the front of the older building. The new building had electric bells and lights, a telephone, drinking fountains, and a motion picture machine. The third floor functioned as an auditorium or two classrooms. The first commencement diploma (12th grade) was issued in 1906. The school complex was demolished in 1939 after sustaining a major fire in 1935.

This group photograph of Jenkintown students was taken in 1912. Subjects taught at the primary level (first through third grades) were reading, arithmetic, spelling, geography, and penmanship. Examinations were held twice a year in December and June. No one could take part in athletics unless they were pupils in good standing and had perfect attendance.

In 1912, a formal athletic program was launched. The first coach, a Mr. Glover, started a baseball team that played in vacant lots until the first athletic field was bought from Thomas Nicholson Jr. on Walnut Street in 1916. Glover also formed and coached the girls' basketball team. From left to right are (first row) E. Waters, E. Friedman, A. Hood, E. Larzalere, K. Tiefenbach, F. Cummings, and E. Coates; (second row) V.A. Ake (faculty), M. Creamer, M. Tailor, E. Borda, G. Wenzell, M. Carson, M. Hahn, M. Mathers, E. Armstrong, and Glover (faculty).

In 1916, the student body launched a publication called the *Red and Blue*. Initially, issues were printed monthly with student-authored articles, including essays, fiction, poetry, humor, and reports on class activities and trips. At the end of the school year, there was a graduation issue. Over time, the publication appeared less frequently until only a graduation issue was published. The name changed after World War II to the *Jenkintownian*, today's yearbook.

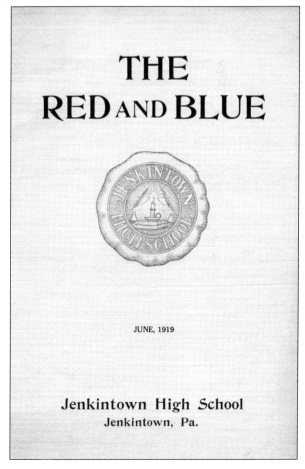

THE
RED AND BLUE

JUNE, 1919

Jenkintown High School
Jenkintown, Pa.

After World War I, the Spaeter home on West Avenue at Spaeter Road (now Highland Avenue) was purchased for a new high school. The architectural firm of Heacock & Hokanson designed the building in 1922, and the first students entered in 1924. A parent-teacher association, now called the Home and School Association, was organized around this time. In 1925, seventh and eighth grades were moved to the high school, and in 1931, two wings were added to the building.

The senior class of 1923 was the last class to graduate from the old West Avenue school building. The class officers were Reese Turner (president), Larry Chadwick (vice president), Mary D. Drumm (secretary), and Ernest Haines (treasurer). There are two African American girls in the second row, Drucilla (second from right) and Jesse Johnson (far right). They were granddaughters of Henry and Jane Porter, who started the Salem Baptist Church in 1884.

Senior-class trips started in 1922, and trip reports were published yearly in the *Red and Blue*. In 1927, the class traveled by train to Washington, DC, and visited the Pan American building, the Bureau of Engraving, and the Washington Monument. The weekend included an evening at the theater and a trip to Mount Vernon. That same year, Jenkintown added a kindergarten for five-year-olds, and the "lifer" tradition started for students attending Jenkintown from kindergarten to 12th grade.

A May Day Festival was held annually on the Highland Avenue athletic field, which had been built in 1930 and dedicated by former Pennsylvania governor Gifford Pinchot. The primary school traditionally staged a royal court, and there was great competition to play the king and queen. The court in the mid-1930s included, from left to right, Jeb Barton (class of 1947), Howard Smith (class of 1948), Edna Scott (queen), and Bill Montgomery (class of 1945). (Jenkintown School District.)

An appreciation for Native American history was taught in the third grade (this being the future class of 1945). The annual educational segment resulted in an extensive and impressive display, including collected artifacts, a model of a village, and exhibited artwork. The 1936 presentation featured the Hopi Indians. (Jenkintown School District.)

Fire destroyed the West Avenue school on February 1, 1935. The loss of the school led to talk of consolidation into a regional school system. This in turn led to community support for an increase in taxes so that a new elementary school could be built. Land was purchased on West Avenue adjacent to the high school. Designed by architect Howell Lewis Shay and funded in part by the Public Works Administration, the new elementary school was ready for occupancy by January 1937.

The class of 1940 celebrated its 25th reunion in April 1965. Elinore S. Miller, a beloved teacher, is in the first row, far left. The class graduates attending include Harold F. Still Jr., Janet Cortright, Madeline Daly, Adele M. Fritsch, Helen Getchell, James Green, Elizabeth Malone, Arthur A. Meder, John Muyskens Jr., Carl Schaffer, and Howard Walton. (Peter Berlinger.)

Boyd Franklin Eckroat (1890–1985) was a self-taught musician and pianist who came to Jenkintown in the 1930s as a music teacher. His daughter Kathleen graduated in 1939. He took leave to serve in World War II but returned in 1945. That year he composed two verses and music for an official Jenkintown "Alma Mater." It was copyrighted and has been sung ever since at school events. Eckroat retired from teaching in 1959. He was also the music director at Grace Presbyterian Church for many years. (Marion Rosenbaum.)

The faculty in 1944 included two teachers who had started teaching before 1930. Nine of these faculty members were still teaching in the early 1960s. The faculty were all college graduates with many holding advanced degrees from notable universities. There was very little turnover of the teaching staff between 1930 and 1960, and several generations in a family were often taught by the same faculty member. Principal Requa W. Bell is in the first row, center. He came to Jenkintown in 1938.

The 1951–1952 men's basketball team, under coach Gerry Palaia and team cocaptains Jack Regan and Jim Watts, won the Class C PIAA All-State Championship. The following season the team won the state title for a second year in a row. The game was played in Reading at Albright College against Centre Hall High with a final score of 88-51. During the season, the team also broke the state scoring record with 139 points in a single game. Following the championship win, the team hoisted Coach Palaia into the air. Team members were Cy Blackfan (captain), brothers Stodie and Eddie Watts, Bob Roy, Dick Solo, Tuck Gordon, Charlie Strauch, Ray Walker, Bill Pyle, and Bill Moore.

The 1954 graduating class posed in front of the main high school entrance just before commencement exercises. Class officers were Richard Solo (president), Marcus Lederman (vice president), Barbara DiJoseph (secretary), and Edward Watts (treasurer). As was and is the Jenkintown tradition, all graduates were dressed formally, and the ladies were given flowers.

The 1955 school play was the comedy *Father Knows Best* (1954). John Rice directed the show, which was his first dramatic production. Rice was a new teacher in 1952 and went on to become principal and then the first school district superintendent. The performance drew a full house. From left to right are Pat Thompson (child), Carol Solo (child), Janet Gruber (mother), Bill Gray (child), and Frank Rossiter (father). Beginning in the mid-1920s, the Dramatic Club staged productions for the community. By 1930, the productions included all high school grades. The tradition continues today.

In 1960, the school board wanted a sign at the entrance to the school. They worked with the high school art teacher, Mildred Weirman, and announced a competition within the school for a design. Cliff Pierce, class of 1960, won the contest, and the school board funded the installation. Over the years, lights have been placed in various places for illumination but the sign remains unchanged. (Jenkintown School District.)

Principal Requa Bell started the Color Day tradition in 1938. Each student from kindergarten to 12th grade was given a color (red or blue), and one day each spring, each grade had their particular game: the kindergartners (orange rush), first graders (farmer and crow), second graders (zigzag), third graders (ring and club relay), fourth graders (under-over relay), fifth graders (bloc shuttle), sixth graders (centipede), seventh graders (obstacle relay), eighth graders (four-way pass), ninth graders (wand relay), tenth graders (pass-back relay), eleventh graders (football relay), and twelfth graders (rope pull). Total points were tallied and a "win" was announced at the end of all competitions. Since 1965, the Color Day bell (from the demolished Baptist church) was painted the winning color. (Tom Tompkins.)

The 1964 commencement included the formally attired graduating class along with a color guard made up of top students in the junior class. For many years, a backdrop helped to set the stage for the ceremony. The high school band provided the music. The school board and superintendent gave out diplomas, scholarships, and awards. (Tom Tompkins.)

In 1964, the school district demolished the Jenkintown Baptist Church and installed new tennis and basketball courts on the site. Following this, a new gymnasium was built where the old tennis courts had been located. A metal plaque was mounted outside the building on the left wall before entering the center doors. It was dedicated to Jenkintown veterans of all wars by the three Jenkintown veterans' organizations: the McKeown-Zane VFW Post, the Coates-Jordan American Legion Post, and the Moore-Triplett American Legion Post.

More school expansion occurred in 1969 with the addition of a cafeteria to the rear of the elementary school that accommodated the entire student body. Before this time, grade school students brought bagged lunches and ate in the grade school gymnasium. Junior and senior high school students could either go home or eat lunch in the high school cafeteria. Presently students do not go home during the school day. (Jenkintown School District.)

In 1952, J. Franklin Kuykendall, a Temple University graduate in music, came to Jenkintown to teach choral music. He was a member of the Pennsylvania Music Educators Association and had many contacts in the Delaware Valley. Under his tenure, many students competed in district, regional, and state choruses. In 1973, the Jenkintown High School Concert Choir joined with the Singing City Youth Choirs in a concert with the Philadelphia Orchestra.

48

After 55 years of use, Jenkintown stadium's aging concrete bleachers were demolished in August 1985 and replaced with a new structure. In preparation for the fall football season, the team returns early before the start of the school year to begin practice for the upcoming season.

Dating back to at least 1938, the school put on an annual Christmas pageant telling the Christmas story. Over the years, the pageant came to be produced by the elementary grades. Students from Margaret Baker's third-grade class perform in the 1982 production. Currently, a holiday or winter concert is presented.

No one remembers when the bonfire tradition started, but it was always held on the Thursday evening before the Friday night homecoming football game. In anticipation of the 1989 bonfire, the community collected wood the week before, and the volunteer fire companies were on alert to put the fire out at the end of the festivities. The tradition ended in 2022 when the decision was made that the bonfire was both too expensive and too risky to continue.

The senior class of 1998 included 17 lifers, meaning those who had attended Jenkintown schools since kindergarten. They are, from left to right, (first row, kneeling) Benjamin Hesse, Steven Lorch, and Kyle Miller; (second row) Kate Lucas, Alison Wortman, Eric Long, Anthony Landy, Chris Richards, Cameron Norbert, Ian Carder, and Mike Monserrat; (third row) Katie Heinz, Noah Marlier, Jason Klein, Emily Link, Robert Brook, and Leslie Hudson.

For many years, Dave Seitz and his fifth-grade students did a history project on Jenkintown entitled Then and Now. In April 1998, the results of that year's efforts were exhibited at the Jenkintown Library. Posterboards displayed many historical images and stories of Jenkintown. Much of the research was done by the students, and the Old York Road Historical Society partnered in the annual endeavor.

Another tradition in Jenkintown is the crowning of a homecoming queen at the football game. At halftime, contestants in convertibles are driven around the track, and the winner is announced over the loudspeakers. In 1997, the tradition was revised, and a homecoming king was also crowned. In 1998, Andrew Fuelleborn and Anna Czulewicz were crowned king and queen. After but two years, tradition resurged, and since then only a queen has been crowned at homecoming. The men have returned to their role as escorts.

In 2001, Kathleen Geer and Carol Shenks cochaired a project to plan, fundraise, and build a community playground located on the grounds of the elementary school. The playground equipment was installed over several very busy community construction days in early October 2002, and at the end of that time, festivities were held to mark the completion. Vertical wooden slats for the fence that encloses the play area are inscribed with the many donor names. (Kieran Farrell.)

A major school facility expansion took place in 2006 when a portion of Highland Avenue at West Avenue was closed and a building connecting the elementary and secondary schools was constructed. Named the Link, the space provides offices and meeting rooms with enhanced security to monitor all visitors.

The 2017–2018 season was a stellar one for the girls' varsity basketball team that went to the Giant Center in Hershey and beat Juniata Valley 51-46 for the PIAA Class IA State Championship. With Jim Romano as longtime coach and Jack Kinnery and Jess Hollinshead as assistant coaches, the winning team included, from left to right (first row) Jennifer Kremp and Amelia Mulvaney; (second row) Carly Mulvaney and Lily Walters; (third row) Ashley Kremp, Mia Kolb, Molly Walsh, Tanner Lafferty, Lauren Brockwell, Courtney Todaro, and Kaitlyn McMahon; (fourth row) Cady Westkaemper, Natalie Kolb, and Caroline Arena. (Jenkintown School District.)

One of the more rewarding duties of the school board each year is to attend the commencement exercises. The 2023 school board included, from left to right (first row) Nancy W. Campbell, Megan O'Brien (president), Kristian Graves, Bridget Reilly Beauchamp, and Katie Costandino; (second row) Patrick Wicks, Lisa Smith, Carolyn Riley (vice president), and Nathan Bridge. (Jenkintown School District.)

The Jenkintown Music Theater got its start in 1945 as a talent show involving a group of parents, teachers, and community members. The goal was and is to raise funds for the school district through the production of a yearly musical. The 1953 cast of *The Fortune Teller* included Frank Kuykendall (the school's new music teacher) as captain of the Royal Hussars and Jack Rice (the new high school principal) as a gypsy musician. Also in this show was Gene Fish (later chairman of the 100th anniversary executive committee in 1974).

The Music Man has been selected three times in the history of the Jenkintown Music Theater (1963, 1982, and 1999). For the 1982 production, Frank and Dolly Kuykendall were musical codirectors, Bob Eyre was the stage director, Jeanne Morris oversaw choreography, and Bill Huttlin was in charge of set design. Cast members included Richard Stevens Sr., Richard Stevens Jr., Chris Stevens, Wendy and Becky Drees, and Shirley and Frank Sweeney. Townspeople included Phil Kuhl and Rob Land. Eleanor Lenz was the dance captain.

The well-known *My Fair Lady* was the 2002 Jenkintown Music Theater production. Cathy Liebars played Eliza Doolittle, Gary Gilbert played Henry Higgins, and Jeff Cline played Freddy Eynsford-Hill. Dancers were Linda Fornicola, Debbie McGoldrick, Christine Meredith, Liz Pope, Sue Roberts, Liza Sheketoff, and Nancy Woehrle.

Frank Kuykendall came to Jenkintown High School in 1952, and his wife, Dolly, after raising their daughter, also joined the faculty. Frank taught music, and Dolly enjoyed a 24-year career teaching English and serving as a guidance counselor. During this time, they were the guiding force of the Jenkintown Music Theater. On April 8, 2006, the school district honored the couple for their valuable contributions and devotion with the naming of the school auditorium, The Kuykendall Auditorium. Frank died later that year, and Dolly followed in 2020.

In October 1912, Dr. Matthew Reaser, formerly of Wilson College, opened a preparatory school and junior college in Jenkintown called the Beechwood School for Young Ladies. The property had previously served as the Beechwood Inn for many years until it fell upon hard times. The Beechwood School renamed the building Beechwood Hall. Certificates were issued in fine arts, music expression, gymnastic education, home economics, domestic arts, and secretaryship. In 1913, an addition was built adding more classrooms and a chapel. (Arcadia University Archives.)

The Beechwood School provided both a finishing school education as well as practical skills training. Home economics was an important part of the curriculum for women at the turn of the 20th century. The course of study involved food preparation and presentation and proper sanitation. Sewing and childcare skills were also part of the home economics program.

Beaver College, founded in 1853 in Beaver County, Pennsylvania, as the Beaver Female Seminary, merged with the Beechwood School in 1925, and by 1926, the combined school had an enrollment of 600. Within a few years, the college purchased the Grey Towers estate in Glenside from the Harrison family, thus giving the school two campuses. Three first-year students arrived on the Jenkintown campus with their suitcases, long capes, hats, and gloves. (Arcadia University Archives.)

In the basement of the main building, now named Beaver Hall, was the Chatterbox, the student snack bar, where students could get food, hear the latest news, and socialize in between classes. All freshmen had to wear green beanie hats from September until November. Whenever passing upperclassmen, a freshman had to tip her hat. Upperclassmen agreed at the November Song Contest to end the hazing period, assuming freshmen performed well in their singing. Hats were then collected to be used for the next year. (Arcadia University Archives.)

The Jenkintown campus of Beaver College was comprised of 11 acres. Beaver Hall is clearly shown in the center. The president's home is in the center, above Beaver Hall on Florence Avenue. The college stables, originally designed for the Beechwood Inn by Horace Trumbauer, are to the left. Jenkintown Elementary School, which was built in 1937, can be seen at the top center. Beaver College operated two campuses until 1962, when the school consolidated to Glenside. The Jenkintown campus was then sold to the Fox brothers, who built Beaver Hill Apartments in 1964. (Arcadia University Archives.)

Four

COMMERCIAL

In January 1897, the view looking up Old York Road toward the center of Jenkintown's commercial district shows that the street was primarily residential until one reached the corner of Greenwood Avenue. There in 1903, the Jenkintown Trust Company would alter the corner building sporting the conical roof. The east side had an open field with a house at the corner of Greenwood Avenue. Trolley tracks ran down the middle of the road; there were no automobiles.

The earliest theater at 212 Old York Road was the Auditorium, established in 1913. From 1919 to 1939, the theater was called the Embassy. The Hiway Theater operated from 1940 to 1988. For a short time in the 1990s, it was called the Merlin. The Hiway was revived in the early 2000s as a nonprofit organization. It later merged into Renew Theaters, which operates several other member-supported nonprofit theaters. The building to the south was designed as an automobile showroom. Butler Buick Company was located here, followed by Scarbrough Motors. Before converting to a microbrewery, the building was home to the Jenkintown Antique Guild from 1976 to 2011.

Flowers were always popular with shoppers in Jenkintown, being essential for proms, commencements, weddings, funerals, and other important celebrations. A.S. Farenwald, a Wyncote resident with greenhouses also there, operated a retail store at the corner of Greenwood Avenue from 1929 to 1959. From the late 1970s until 2006, the Dinette & Sleep Shop was located here. In the 2000s, the building was stripped back to its original exterior configuration of a Colonial-era house.

The northeast corner of Old York Road and Greenwood Avenue in 1951 featured a taxi stand, Towne Men's Shop, and Shaff's Furniture Store, which also repaired antiques and did upholstery. The building was the former Nice Brothers undertaking establishment and was one of the oldest buildings in Jenkintown when it was demolished in 2002 to make room for parking and outside dining for the Drake Tavern.

Looking north on Old York Road above Greenwood Avenue around 1947 highlights automobile parking along both sides of the street. This state of affairs lasted until the 1970s, when PennDOT took over maintenance of the roadway and eliminated on-street parking to accommodate traffic volume. The businesses south of the bank on the east side of York Road were all built after the Cottman House was razed in 1923.

The Cottman family purchased the Sarah Jenkins Hotel in 1834 and operated the inn for many years. In 1879, the Cottmans constructed a new hotel and tavern just north of the inn and demolished the older building when the new establishment was complete. The Cottman House stood at what is today the northeast corner of Old York Road and West Avenue. During Prohibition, the "B" in "Beer" was removed from both the sign over the door and the sign on the porch roof facing Old York Road. To the rear of the building, horse auctions were held in later years.

In July 1922, the Jenkintown National Bank, founded in 1875, and the Jenkintown Trust Company, founded in 1903, merged to form the Jenkintown Bank and Trust Company. Six months later, the bank announced the purchase of the Cottman House for the construction of a new bank. Designed by architect Horace Trumbauer and occupied on November 4, 1925, the new building proclaimed the bank's status as the largest suburban financial institution in the vicinity of Philadelphia. Through many mergers and name changes, Wells Fargo Bank closed the branch around 2018.

Throughout World War II, nylon stockings were unavailable due to the war effort. Following the end of hostilities, nylon stockings made a return but the demand was great, as seen in the winter of 1945 with a long line of mostly women queuing at the Cedar Chest, a small clothing store at 441 Old York Road, next door to Horn & Hardart. Launched in Philadelphia, Horn & Hardart's developed the automat, the first self-service restaurant. By 1941, the concern operated 157 shops in the Philadelphia, New York, and Baltimore areas.

A Sears store first opened in Jenkintown at 414 Old York Road in 1931. Its popularity soon led to the construction in 1935 of a new and larger store at the corner of Old York and Homestead Roads. A year after suffering a fire in 1957, Sears moved to Abington where Target is now located. This site then became home to a Rambler automobile showroom.

The Jenkintown Bowling Alleys was renamed T-Bird Bowling when it moved from its Johnson Street quarters that had been destroyed in a 1957 fire. Originally constructed as a Food Fair supermarket in 1938, the building at 440 Old York Road opened on July 1, 1960. The space had been completely renovated to accommodate 14 bowling alleys. T-Bird remained until 1985, when it relocated to Willow Grove as Thunderbird Lanes. The building was demolished in 1988 to make way for Summersgate, an assisted living facility that was later renamed Chelsea. The building is presently unoccupied.

In 1955, the former Kelly mansion was razed, and the Avenue of the Shops opened with Bonwit Teller as the anchor tenant. The arcade operated until 1972, when Bloomingdale's took over the entire strip and added a second floor to the length of the structure. After 1982 when a number of area department stores moved to the Willow Grove Park mall, successor occupants of this space were Nutrisystem and Zany Brainy. It is now occupied mostly by medical offices.

Designed by the architectural firm of Dreher & Churchman, the Jenkintown location of Strawbridge & Clothier's department store was built in 1931. Being the first outpost along the Old York Road of a major center-city department store, the new suburban location established Jenkintown as a shopping mecca for many years. The store also hosted many local groups, including the Old York Road Art Guild and the Old York Road Garden Club.

With a booming business, Strawbridge & Clothier made the decision in 1953 to expand its building, nearly doubling its size and adding a sizable parking deck to the north. Alas, like Sears and Bloomingdales, Strawbridge & Clothier left in 1982 for the Willow Grove Park mall. The building now has many shops, including an Outback Steakhouse, legal offices, a storage facility, and a nursing school. The Art Deco building was added to the National Register of Historic Places in 1989.

Howard Johnson's started business in 1925 in Massachusetts and by the 1950s was the largest restaurant chain in the United States. Jenkintown's restaurant operated for a short time prior to World War II. The eatery was located on the corner of Old York Road and Washington Lane, with the property running from Cedar Street around to Harper Avenue.

By 1941, Williamson's restaurant had moved into the former Howard Johnson's location. In 1946, it expanded its dining facilities. A disastrous fire at lunchtime on January 31, 1961, forced 250 diners out and the business to relocate to Horsham. The parcel was subdivided, and an office building, oil changing facility, and a dry cleaner now occupy the site.

Looking north along Old York Road above Harper Avenue, the Acme Markets store opened in 1941, along with a new building for Jackson-Cross realtors. A few buildings up is an A&P supermarket. A&P had several prior locations in Jenkintown before moving to this new store in 1948. The supermarket completely renovated the building in 1964 but would be gone by the end of the decade.

Martin's Aquarium was a Jenkintown landmark on Old York Road at the northwest corner of Harper Avenue. Begun in northwest Philadelphia by Martin Weintraub, the store relocated to Jenkintown in 1971 and suffered a disastrous fire in 1973. Billed as the "world's largest aquarium," Martin's closed in 1997. It was an enjoyable place to bring children to observe the fish, listen to the birds, and pet the puppies. It is now a mattress store.

Looking southwest on York Road from Greenwood Avenue, the Philadelphia Suburban Gas and Electric Company operated in a building constructed in 1917 at the northwest corner of York Road and Summit Avenue. The building was later home to Sack's Jewelers, which closed during the COVID pandemic. Farther north, Larmon Camera Shop operated at 211 York Road from 1939 until moving to the Avenue of the Shops in 1956. On the corner at Greenwood Avenue is the Service Center Building, which was constructed in 1899 as a boy's club but evolved from a civic space into a commercial and office structure.

The Unity Frankford store on the north side of Greenwood Avenue was located in the building that was home to the Jenkintown Trust Company since it was founded in 1903. After the bank merged in 1922, a variety of stores occupied the ground floor. Since 1968 and now spanning three generations, Edelman's Coins has been based here. To the north was the W.C. Fleck & Bro. Hardware store. The multigenerational Fleck business started in 1865 and moved to this site in the mid-1870s. The previous Fleck building was consumed in a spectacular fire in 1933. A new fireproof building arose. Fleck's owned a number of buildings in the borough and operated many supply-related concerns, including tire, harness, and stable supplies and a manufacturing business. The latter relocated to Willow Grove when Jenkintown refused to allow the expansion of its production facility.

In 1948, the hardware and building supply business of W.C. Fleck gave way to B.E. Block & Bro. Inc. (Fleck's retail division). The store sold housewares, toys, and sporting goods. A Sun Ray Drug Store was to the north. This building previously served as an American Stores location and Woolworth's. The Goldberg building was designed by architect T. Walton Heiss and constructed in 1922. Heiss was also the architect of the 1934 Fleck building.

Morris Goldberg started his clothing business in 1902 on Greenwood Avenue before moving to West Avenue. In 1922, the store expanded into a new building on Old York Road. Many Jenkintown residents remember shopping in this store during the two world wars when money was tight and credit was extended. Goldberg retired in 1959. His store was considered the oldest department store along the Old York Road. Several generations of his family still live in the area. (They are not related to the Goldbergs of the television series.)

The Jenkintown House or Bellis Hotel was located on the southwest corner of Old York Road and West Avenue. Originally the site of a general store from the 1770s to 1850, the property became a tavern and then a hotel. Prior operators included Joseph Stemple, Thomas Fetter, and George van Dyke, and in the 1860s, it was known as the Phoenix Hotel. By the time the building was demolished, the ground floor had reverted to a meat and produce store.

F.W. Woolworth Company was first located at 311 Old York Road next to Morris Goldberg's store beginning in 1927. In 1948, Woolworths moved to a new building at the southwest corner of Old York Road and West Avenue. There it remained until around 1980, to be followed by a long succession of businesses, including Linens Unlimited, Cook's Connections gourmet kitchen store, a dance studio, and a bridal shop. The building was heavily altered in 1989 but has since been remodeled to look more like the 1948 design.

The Foy Building stood on the northwest corner of Old York Road and West Avenue. Furman T. Foy was a jeweler from 1905 to 1910. The family house stood immediately to the rear of the building. Over the years, several other businesses were located at this site, including a newsstand, a dentist, and a grocery store. In 1919, Foy was also in the real estate and brokerage business. The Foy family would later have a car dealership in the Jenkintown area.

The Oswald Drug Store purchased the Foy Building in 1946 and had it demolished for a modern structure. The drugstore previously operated on the 300 block of Old York Road from the 1930s to 1946. In the 1960s, Marvin Weiser bought Oswald's pharmacy but did not change the name. The pharmacy closed in 2014. The building was most recently occupied by Sparrow and Hawk, a clothing store.

Looking south on Old York Road from Homestead Road in the early 1920s, the west side of the street is on the cusp of major changes. The bank building on the right is the Jenkintown National Bank, first located just south of the Masonic Temple from 1875 to 1878 and then moved to 411 Old York Road, where it was in operation from 1878 to 1922. It was demolished in the late 1920s to make way for the Yorkway Place group of stores. Additional buildings south of the bank were constructed in 1926. A Montgomery clothing store was located there for many years.

Mr. Paul's barbershop traces its roots back to 1915 when Bill Cornelius started in business in a shop adjoining Clayton's store and pool hall at the corner of Greenwood Avenue and Cedar Street. Cornelius moved the barbershop to 310 York Road in 1920 and turned the business over to Bill Closson in 1945. Paul Strate joined Closson in 1962, and in 1971, Closson retired and gave the business to Strate. Strate moved the shop in 1980 to its present location at 415 Old York Road. He was honored at a Jenkintown Town Square celebration for his then 60 years in business. (Paul Strate.)

The west side of the 400 block of Old York Road around 1950 featured Alan Hosiery, Pliner Shoes, Jack and Jill's, Wille's Children Shop, and the Masonic Temple. Carlson Motors, Chrysler-Plymouth dealers, occupied both the north and south corners of Cherry Street. Farther on were a number of additional businesses, ending at the Medical Arts Building at the southwest corner of Hillside Avenue.

A Singer Sewing Machine Company retail store originally opened on Yorkway Place in 1938, but it soon moved to 469 Old York Road. On May 2, 1949, the store held a fashion show that packed the house. By 1961, the store had moved to Willow Grove.

In 1925, the employees of the A&P gathered in their grocery store located at 715 West Avenue. By the 1930s, the store was located at 433 Old York Road, and in 1948, it would move to a new building just south of Summit Avenue.

From 1941 to 1974, the Jenkintown-Abington Federal Savings & Loan was located at 705 West Avenue. Founded at the Phoenix Hotel as the Abington Building Association, the name changed after the association received a federal charter in 1956. The bank moved to 415 Old York Road in 1974 but soon left for a new corporate headquarters at 180 Old York Road in Abington. After several name changes, Abington Bank converted to stock in 2004 and was taken over by Susquehanna Bank in 2011.

W.C. Fleck's grandson J. Frank Fleck opened his own hardware business starting in the mid-1930s. In 1950, the store moved to 99 West Avenue, where it remained until it closed in 1985. John and Peggy Ewer purchased the business from Fleck and ran it for many years.

Humphrey's Gas Station, pumping gas from the Atlantic Refining Company, operated on the northwest corner of West Avenue and Maple Street from 1934 until at least 1950. The building is now a multifamily apartment, and the gas station is long gone.

A. Jackson Smith and Samuel L. Schively started a coal, lumber, and feed business, Smith & Schively, in 1894. They sold corn, oats, bran, baled hay and straw, lime, flagstone, curb and paving stone, plaster hair, cement, bar sand, coal, lumber, and kindling wood. Later known simply as the Schively Lumber Yard, the business was located at 99 West Avenue near the train tracks. Behind the business along the tracks were cabins that housed several black families, some of whose members worked at the lumberyard. In December 1930, the yard suffered a disastrous fire. In 1989, the office building 101 West Avenue was constructed on the site.

Walker Cadillac relocated to the corner of West and Greenwood Avenues around 1940. The Webb Cadillac dealership later took over the site. In 1966, Webb Cadillac moved to the Fairway in Abington, and the structure was demolished the following year to make way for the Jenkintown Plaza office building, which was designed by the architectural firm of Evantash & Friedman. In 1964, the Fox brothers were building Beaver Hill Apartments overlooking the dealership.

The Triangle Cleaning and Dyeing Establishment was founded in 1913 and operated at 609 Summit Avenue. The business also had an office in Mount Airy at Stenton and Mount Pleasant Avenues for several years. In 2005, the property was sold and general contractor Jeff Lustig later renovated the building into apartments. The dry-cleaning business was sold and relocated to West Chelten Avenue in Philadelphia.

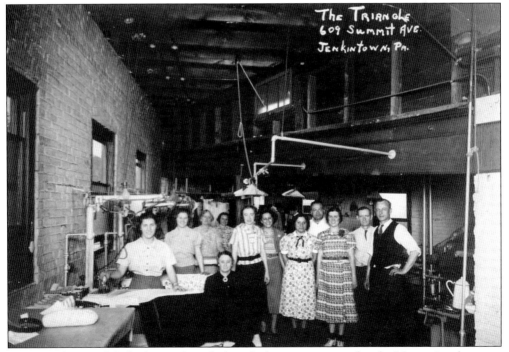

Triangle Cleaning did all of its work, including the business generated at the Mount Airy location, in the Jenkintown plant. The employees gathered for a group photograph, with a number of the ladies stationed at their ironing boards. George A. Wall was manager in 1932, followed by M.M. Abbott in 1933.

The Jenkintown Water Company was chartered in 1889. Artesian wells were drilled in Wyncote, and two water towers (sandpipes) were built to hold 100,000 gallons of water. Underground pipes were laid throughout the town. The company's office and sandpipes stood at the northwest corner of Summit Avenue and Leedom Street. The elevated tower, built in 1894, was moved to Fort Dix in New Jersey in 1917. The water tower was one of the Jenkintown landmarks that was featured in the fictional Jenkintown-related television series *The Goldbergs*, which ran from 2013 to 2023. The water company sold the property in 1979 for development.

The Jenkintown Water Company merged with the Moreland Spring Water Company by 1911 and then with the Philadelphia Water Company around 1922 to become the Philadelphia Suburban Water Company. By then, water was being pumped from Pennypack Creek in Bethayres to water towers on Edge Hill Road in Abington, with the wells and pumping station in Jenkintown and Wyncote abandoned. The company continued to maintain an office in Jenkintown, acquiring the former Supplee-Wills-Jones Milk Company building in 1954. In 1996, the water company sold its building to Salem Baptist Church.

Paul Jaeger sold hunting and sports equipment. The firm was widely known for its custom-built rifles. The business was active from the late 1940s until 1985. Located at 209 Leedom Street, the site today is home to Painting With a Twist. The store runs alongside the rear of the former Jenkintown Hobby Center, which started in 1951 and moved into this new building in 1958. When the original owner of the hobby shop sold the business in 1978, he gave the building to Jenkintown Youth Activities. The hobby shop continued until 1999.

Andrew S. Argue started in 1885 dealing in used furniture. His son Arthur C. joined him after World War I, and they built the property at 209 Leedom Street, where they made reproduction furniture for the big estates in the area, employing four cabinetmakers and two upholsterers. They lost the building during the Depression but moved to 443 Leedom Street. Arthur Jr. joined the business following World War II. The business continued until he retired in 1999.

The north side of Greenwood Avenue in the 600 block was occupied by several businesses in 1945. The welding and blacksmith shop was owned by Reese Flower. W. John Stevens was located next door. Next door at the corner was a laundry, although the business was closed by this time. The laundry building is now Olive Lucy. The remaining structures down to the Independence Fire Company were demolished when the Immaculate Conception school and parking lot were built in the 1960s.

Reese W. Flower (1882–1958), pictured working at his forge in November 1945, was a wheelwright and blacksmith. The business was started in the 1890s by his father, Richard Flower, who was also involved in building carriages in the first decade of the 1900s. The firm was located at 613 Greenwood Avenue. By the early 1920s, the firm was sherardizing ironworks and, by the 1930s, doing welding work. Flower retired around 1950.

In 1938, Joseph Stutz started making candy in his garage at 457 Leedom Street. Following World War II and business success, he purchased the former Clayton's cigar store at the corner of Greenwood Avenue and Cedar Street. In 1956 and 1958, branches of Stutz's Candies were opened in Ship Bottom, New Jersey, and Warrington, respectively. In 1965, the business was sold to John Glaser. Candy-making operations moved to Hatboro in 1976. The store eventually closed in 2012, and the building was demolished for parking in 2014.

Designed by Philadelphia architect Philip S. Tyre in 1927, the building was erected for Walker Cadillac as a showroom and service station. By the mid-1930s, it was home to the H.L. Peterson Oldsmobile dealership. The building was located at 707 Greenwood Avenue on the site of the original Fleck family home. The building was demolished for parking in 1998 and is now part of the Jenkintown Town Square complex.

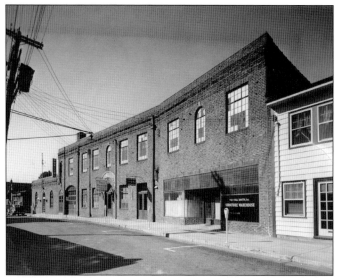

The *Chronicle* was founded on March 28, 1894, and a week later, the *Jenkintown Times* was founded by William Clayton and his brother Levi. In December, the papers merged to form the *Times-Chronicle*. When Clayton died in 1918, his wife, Gertrude, took over the paper and ran it until 1936, when it was purchased by William Potter Wear, George H. Bennett, and Howard R. Yoder. Gertrude moved the newspaper from 413 Old York Road into a new building at 421 Johnson Street in 1927.

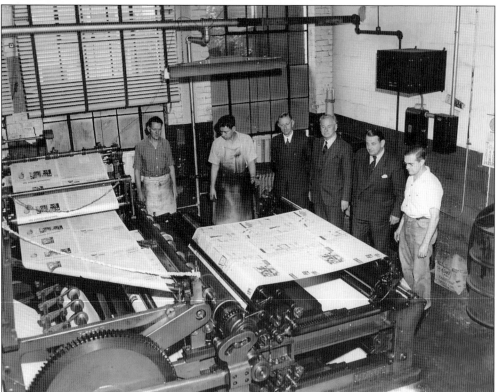

The Times-Chronicle Publishing Company owned and printed several weekly newspapers in addition to the *Times-Chronicle*. In the pressroom on September 27, 1950, are pressmen Al Randall (left) and Joe Tull (second from left). Prior to offset press printing, the newspaper was printed on a letterpress that employed manual typesetting. In 1959, the company merged with Montgomery Publishing Company. By 1983, with printing operations moving to Fort Washington, the newspaper staff took up smaller quarters at 466 Johnson Street. All operations consolidated to Fort Washington in 1999.

The Jenkintown Bowling Recreation Company occupied the second floor of the Times-Chronicle Building, with an entrance at 417 Johnson Street. The bowling alley was popular and well-patronized. The business moved to Old York Road after a 1957 fire destroyed its space. The fire started when the bowling alley was refinishing its lanes using flammable substances.

Photographer Harry J. Utzy (1908–1992) was a local Jenkintown boy who grew up on Leedom Street and 410 West Avenue. He turned his hobby into a lifetime career. His office was located on Old York Road and then at 516 Cedar Street before moving to 435 Johnson Street in the early 1950s. The building had previously been the Hanloh's Custom Cosmetics and Hairdressing shop. When Utzy retired in the late 1980s, he donated his entire collection to the Old York Road Historical Society. Since 1990, the building has been home to the Jenkintown Chiropractic Center.

The Yorkway Diner was located on West Avenue near Cottman Street. The diner opened in 1939. In 1955, with the diner long gone, the adjoining house was purchased by the Jenkintown Parking Corporation, and the area was cleared to make way for parking spaces. From the 1920s on, parking in Jenkintown's business district, or the lack thereof, was a perennial issue facing the borough and the local shop owners.

The Herkness building at the corner of Homestead Road and Cottman Street was designed by the architectural firm of Seeburger & Rabenold in 1928 as six offices, each with its own entrance. Wayne and Malcolm Herkness were two brothers whose firm was both a realtor and developer. They were largely responsible for all of the pre–World War II development of Rydal and Meadowbrook. Commonwealth Land Company and the Land & Title Company maintained offices at this location to facilitate real estate settlements.

Five

CHURCHES

The first church built in Jenkintown was the Church of Our Saviour in 1858. The Episcopal church was funded with a $10,000 contribution and on land donated by William H. Newbold, who lived at Vernon, the former Stephen Jenkins home. A rectory was constructed in 1861, and a school building was erected five years later. Between 1890 and 1906, the sanctuary building was enlarged several times. In 2019, the congregation sold its buildings and met jointly with St. John's Church in Huntingdon Valley before formally merging in 2022.

Homestead Hall, the church's parish house, was built in 1893 on the plans of architectural firm Furness & Evans. In 1937, the building was modified and enlarged by architect Marmaduke Tilden. When a local Jenkintown developer purchased the church property in 2019, the sanctuary building and Homestead Hall were repurposed. The rectory and garage were torn down in 2023, and a mixed-use apartment building should be ready for occupancy in 2024.

In 1943, during World War II, the entire parish house was turned into a service center for the men and women in the nation's armed services. The Church Door Canteen operated for two years, and hospitality was extended by the entire Jenkintown community. Service personnel mostly came from the Willow Grove Air Base and the Philadelphia Naval Ship Yard. The Canteen was open daily, and dances were held several nights a week. A library, snack bar, and many games were among the diversions extended to those in service.

The Immaculate Conception Church was built in 1866 on land purchased from William and Helena Cottman on the southeast corner of West Avenue and Cedar Street. The Roman Catholic congregation started with 100 parishioners from many surrounding areas. Father Toner, a 26-year-old from Ireland, was the first priest. The interior of the first church shows electrical lighting installed at Eastertide in 1894. Fr. Joseph A. Strahan, pastor from 1892 until 1915, officiated at that time.

In 1928, a fire gutted the sanctuary building, which was rumored to have been started by the Ku Klux Klan from the Hatboro area. This group had demonstrated on the steps of the church the previous year with hate threats against the Pope. Work began almost immediately on a new building, which was dedicated in September 1929. However, Fr. John E. Cavanaugh, who personally endured both the night of the fire and the exhausting efforts to raise the funds for rebuilding, declined in health and died several months before the dedication.

Cardinal J. Dougherty dedicated the new church edifice on September 22, 1929, assisted by the congregation's new priest, Thomas F. McNally. To the left is the rectory, and to the right is the former convent, which now serves as offices.

Immaculate Conception was able to launch a parochial school in 1895. A school building was erected on Cedar Street behind the rectory. The school was headed by Fr. Joseph A. Strahan, who conducted classes with two other lay teachers. In 1898, Father Strahan invited the Sisters of St. Joseph of Chestnut Hill to join the faculty. The rectory was modified for the Sisters' use, and a new rectory was constructed on the east side of the church.

Father Strahan stands with the second-grade class in 1912 on the front steps of the church. Margaret Green, a well-known student, is identified on the second row, second from left. Father Cavanagh added a second floor to the school building as enrollment continued to increase. The structure was demolished in 1967 after a new school building had opened.

Father McNally added a new school to the east of the rectory. The architects were Peter F. Getz and Paul W. Getz, and the builder was Joseph R. Farrell. The school building opened in November 1966. In 1988, the Sisters of St. Joseph withdrew from teaching, and lay teachers were hired. The school operated until 2012 when the Archdiocese of Philadelphia merged it with St. Luke's School in Glenside to form St. Joseph the Protector regional Catholic school. A preschool for ages two and up operates at the Jenkintown site.

Early Methodist meetings were held from the 1830s in the Jenkinstown Lyceum building. When the Abington Public Schools went to auction its old public school building at the corner of Leedom Street and West Avenue, three Methodist men won the public auction, and the Jenkintown United Methodist Church was born. In the late 1890s, the church decided to move to a more residential neighborhood, and the building was sold to the borough in 1901.

A new Methodist church was dedicated in 1902 at the southwest corner of Summit Avenue and Walnut Street. George Fleck, B.W. Fleck, and W.C. Fleck were neighbors and active church members living on both Walnut Street and Summit Avenue. The family's properties on both sides of the church were later acquired by the church when expansion was necessary for the growing congregation.

In 1950, the adjoining house on Summit Avenue was purchased to accommodate the church school. From 1952 to 1954, the church building was extensively remodeled. During construction, services were held at nearby Beaver College. To the left, the parsonage built at 143 Walnut Street housed several of the church's ministers for many years, but it is presently providing rental income.

In 1960, Fellowship House on Summit Avenue was demolished, and a new educational building was constructed, opening in 1963. Today, the hall houses a church school and provides additional space for community activities. A preschool group named JUMP (Jenkintown United Methodist Preschool), founded by Penny Riggs, has provided day care services for many years and is still active. The Jenkintown Food Cupboard also operates out of this location.

The Reverend Robert Steele, the pastor of Abington Presbyterian Church, started prayer services at the Jenkinstown Lyceum in 1845. His successor, Samuel T. Lowrie, continued this work and joined with John Wanamaker, a prominent Philadelphia Presbyterian who had a summer home nearby, to purchase a lot in Jenkintown and build a chapel. In 1881, Grace Presbyterian Church became an independent congregation from Abington.

In 1906, the Presbyterian congregation commissioned Horace Trumbauer, a local Jenkintown architect who had grown up on Hillside Avenue, to build twin buildings on Old York Road across from the church. The northern twin served as the manse to house the church's minister. The southern twin brought in rental income for many years. The church sold the twin residences in later years, and the proceeds funded the construction of a new manse on Vista Road.

In 1926–1927, the Presbyterian congregation constructed a large Sunday school building behind the church sanctuary. By 1953, membership was over 1,000, and fundraising began in earnest to enlarge the sanctuary. E. Allen Reeves, Inc. of Abington, was the builder. During the renovation, services were held in the Sunday school building auditorium.

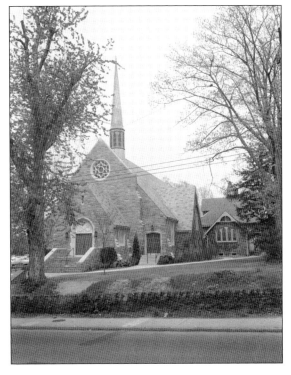

The enlarged church was dedicated in April 1956. Many other changes were to come, but the exterior has not changed since 1956. In the 1970s, the congregation was active in supporting Rydal Park, a new continuing-care retirement community. Today, Grace Presbyterian Church has embarked on a capital fund drive to upgrade its facilities. The goal is to further increase its presence in serving the needs of the Jenkintown community.

In 1880, Jenkintown Baptist Church was organized. The nascent congregation was gifted a lot at the southwest corner of Walnut Street and West Avenue where a church was erected and dedicated on November 1, 1883. In 1922, an adjoining Sunday school building was constructed. In the late 1950s, a school-release program operated from the church for children in first through eighth grades. The program ended with a US Supreme Court decision regarding the separation of church and state.

In 1960, under the Reverend Charles Woodson, the Jenkintown Baptist congregation merged with the Tioga Baptist Church to form Abington Baptist Church. The new congregation continued to worship in Jenkintown while awaiting the completion of a new facility on Huntingdon Road in Abington. After the dedication of the new church in March 1963, the school district purchased the corner property and demolished the church in 1964. Jenkintown School District inherited the church bell, and it was moved to the football field; it is now the Color Day bell.

Salem Baptist Church was organized in 1884. In 1889, the church purchased a lot on Summit Avenue at Leedom Street. The first building was a wooden structure that was replaced by a brick structure that served from 1909 until 1957. In 1959, a new church edifice was dedicated, and in 1980, the adjacent home was demolished for a Christian education center. In 1996, the church purchased the adjoining Philadelphia Suburban Water Company building and converted it into a family life center. In 2019, the congregation moved to a more spacious campus in Roslyn, and the church property was cleared for an apartment building called Summit House.

The Reverend Robert Johnson-Smith Sr. was a Morehouse College graduate and classmate of the Reverend Martin Luther King Jr. Smith served as pastor of Salem from 1956 until his retirement in 1996. He invited Dr. King to Jenkintown more than once, and after one visit, King donated his honorarium for a stained glass window. Other prominent civil rights leaders also visited Salem, including Leon Sullivan, Jesse Jackson, Rosa Parks, Andrew Young, and William Gray.

In 1971, Salem Baptist Church purchased the property at 309 Walnut Street from the Dabney Vest family, longtime church members. The goal was to build affordable housing available to all regardless of race, color, or creed. Overcoming many obstacles, the SALBA Apartments, built in 1972, is comprised of 17 units for lower-income families and the elderly. (Marion Rosenbaum.)

Christian Scientists first held services in Jenkintown in 1933. By 1936, land was purchased, and architect W. Pope Barney was selected to design a church in the Colonial style. Located at the northwest corner of Washington Lane and Newbold Road, the church opened in 1937. The Reading Room was located on Yorkway Place for many years. In 2017, the church building was purchased by the Vision of Hope Baptist Church. The Christian Science Church and Reading Room now rent space in the Jenkintown Metroplex on the 400 block of Old York Road.

Six

CHARITABLE
AND CULTURAL

The Abington Library Society occupied space in the Masonic Hall from 1878 until 1910, inhabiting several spaces within the building over that period. Its final room, pictured here in 1905, was on the second floor. John W. Ridpath was instrumental in bringing the library into the building, as he was an officer in the Masonic lodge as well as a building tenant with his drugstore. In 1903, the library celebrated its 100th anniversary by making itself open to the public without charge. Previously, one needed to be a member to access the collection.

The Abington Library Society purchased the Jenkinstown Lyceum building in 1909, and architect Charles L. Borie incorporated the structure into a new library edifice in the Greek Revival style thanks to the generosity of financier Clement B. Newbold. Newbold's gift was in memory of his young wife, the former Mary D. Scott, who died after a routine appendectomy in 1905. She was the daughter of Thomas A. Scott, president of the Pennsylvania Railroad.

Shortly after the library building was completed, another major gift was received from the estate of artist John Lambert Jr. (1861–1907). Lambert attended the Pennsylvania Academy of Fine Arts and the University of Pennsylvania. He painted portraits and landscapes and lived with his parents at their estate Aysgarth, just below the Abington Presbyterian Church. His bequest enabled the construction of an addition to the library in memory of his father. The Lambert Room still contains family furniture and portraits, some of which Lambert painted.

Florence May Ridpath (1868–1961) was the daughter of Rachel F. and John W. Ridpath and grew up with three brothers and two sisters on Walnut Street just north of West Avenue. She attended West Chester State Normal School, became a librarian in 1902, and served for 43 years as Jenkintown's librarian, presiding over the circulation desk in the main room of the library until she retired. (Jenkintown Library.)

Lucille Wallower (1910–1999) studied at the Pennsylvania Museum School of Art and then became a librarian for the Harrisburg Public Library. She was best known as a children's book author specializing in Pennsylvania history. She came to Jenkintown as a children's librarian in 1959, became head librarian in 1972, and retired in 1976. The library staff in 1971 included, from left to right, (first row) Edith Prout, Shirley Cressman, Kay Whismer, Lucille Wallower, and Marion Blamberg; (second row) Esther Fry, Marge Chalfont, and Jane Walker. (Jenkintown Library.)

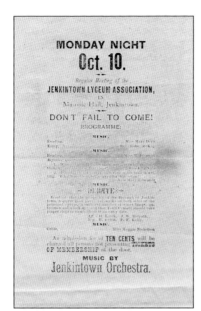

During the latter part of the 19th century, there were a number of cultural organizations active in Jenkintown. The Jenkintown Lyceum Association, a rival to the moribund (at that time) Jenkinstown Lyceum, met in the Masonic Hall and hosted any number of events. One evening's musical program included music by the Jenkintown Orchestra, interspersed with readings, and a debate over whether paved sidewalks, lighting, patrolmen, and a lockup were required for the town's prosperity.

Located at the southwest corner of Greenwood Avenue and York Road, the Jenkintown Club House and Reading Rooms was erected by William West Frazier in 1899 on the design of the Philadelphia architectural firm of Furness, Evans & Company for the use of Jenkintown's men and boys. Frazier was in the sugar refining business, and he and his family were longtime members of Church of Our Saviour. In 1924, the building became known as the Old York Road Service Centre, although it was still owned by Frazier. Many of Jenkintown's civic, social, and cultural organizations were based in the building at one time or another. Rental income supported the Episcopal church for many years until the building was sold by the Frazier Trust.

Annie W. and Theodore B. Culver lived in the early 1900s at Florence and Greenwood Avenues. They were longtime members of Grace Presbyterian Church. In 1903, several young black children were found in a barn on Summit Avenue while their parents were at work. Annie contacted the Reverend S.J. Jones of Salem Baptist Church for assistance, and a Jenkintown Day Nursery was formed with Annie as its first head. The first year, the borough offered its lockup as space for the nursery. Cecilia D. Potter from the Salem Baptist Church volunteered her services as the first teacher.

What started as an all-black nursery in the beginning soon became an integrated group. In 1928, the children are shown at the nursery building at Thomas and Water Streets, which was its location for many years. In 1965, the school moved to Abington at Baeder and Hilltop Roads. In 2015, an agreement was reached with Play and Learn, a Montgomery County nonprofit group with multiple day care centers, to manage the operation.

During World War I, the Ogontz and Huntingdon Valley Branch of the American Red Cross was organized. In May 1918, the branch occupied the house on the southeast corner of Old York Road and Greenwood Avenue. Many socially prominent ladies of the area were involved in the running and work of the organization. By 1928, the group had joined with other similar organizations and the Old York Road branch of the Southeastern Pennsylvania Chapter of the American Red Cross emerged.

As the Old York Road branch of the Red Cross grew, new facilities were required. Local architect John A. Bower modified the 1866 building that was the former home of several prominent Jenkintownians into a new headquarters. A ribbon cutting was held in January 1950. In 1988, the building was sold to be converted into apartments. Across the street, the Victorian structure on the north side of West Avenue was owned by the McGoldrick family at the time it was demolished in 1993 to make way for an apartment building.

Over the years, a number of Scouting troops have been based in Jenkintown. In 1950, Cub Scout Pack No. 13 held a father-and-son dinner. From Den 4 are, from left to right, Cub Scouts Rick Jackson, Paul Moody, Berk MacKenney, Joe Kiefner, Bill Gray, Bill Haines, and Sandy Diamond, with their fathers standing behind them. There were also two Boy Scout troops in Jenkintown. These groups disbanded in the 1980s and 1990s.

Cub Scout Pack 210 operates out of Grace Presbyterian Church. Attending the Pack 210 banquet in February 2000 are, from left to right, Robert Sobeck, Sean Reiley, den leader Peggy Salvatore, and Ben Heidorn. In 2001, Cubmaster Bob Gabage founded Boy Scout Troop 201 in order to keep the boys in Jenkintown as there was no Jenkintown-based Boy Scout troop at that time. Troop 201 is affiliated with the Immaculate Conception Church.

The Rotary Club of Jenkintown was chartered in 1924 as the first civic-minded service club in the borough. While the club presently meets at Grace Presbyterian Church, for many years the club held its weekly luncheon meetings in the clubhouse of the Old York Road Country Club (now the Abington Club). Between 1925 and 1967, the club founded six other area Rotary Clubs.

In May 1982, twenty-seven past presidents of the Rotary Club of Jenkintown gathered for a group photograph. Among them are Jenkintownians Arthur Argue, Paul Cutright, Wally Gordon, Bill Lange, Bob Lloyd, Luther Kauffman, John Rice, Lou Riggs, Don Walton, and Charles Zerbe. Women were admitted into the club in 1989.

For a number of years, the Rotary Club's major fundraisers have been a citrus fruit sale in the winter and a pancake breakfast in the spring. In 2016, the club's 11th annual breakfast was held in the Muyskens auditorium of Grace Presbyterian Church, at which time it raised over $10,000. Breakfast entertainment includes many of the musical groups at the Jenkintown schools. (Jenkintown Rotary Club.)

With the funds it raises, the Rotary Club donates grants to local nonprofit organizations and awards scholarships to Jenkintown High School seniors. Recent grant recipients include the Jenkintown Library, the Jenkintown High School music program, the Jenkintown High School World Language Society, the League of Women Voters, the Breathing Room Foundation, and the Old York Road Historical Society. (Jenkintown Rotary Club.)

The Old York Road Symphony was founded in 1933 by Louis Angeloty, who had been in the first violin section of the Philadelphia Orchestra; Suzanne C. Meder of the Jenkintown School of Cultural Arts; and Stanley Chute of the theater orchestra of the Old York Road Players. Early rehearsals were held in the Service Center Building. At a rehearsal in the fall of 1954, Angeloty reviews a score with, from left to right, Arlene Gerstenfeld, Kay Hoover, Ann Sturgeon, Russell Hill, and Matthew Ehrlich.

The second conductor of the orchestra was Wolfgang B. Richter, here conducting a 1960 rehearsal. Jenkintown players that can be identified are Fred H. Bates (violin), Bill Yick (cello), and Suzanne C. Meder (violin). Richter left in 1968 and was followed by Joseph Primavera, a violist with the Philadelphia Orchestra. In 1978, Mark Laycock was conductor. Arne Running came in 1984 and served until 1997. Several more conductors have followed, including Jack Moore, the current maestro.

The Old York Road Women's Exchange opened in 1932 as a nonprofit consignment store. The next year it found rental space at 429 Johnson Street. It conducted a store as well as a tea room and restaurant. In addition to its annual fundraisers, the women organized garden tours, bridge tournaments, and a book lecture subscription series. After World War II, an economy shop replaced the restaurant selling inexpensive used clothing, bedspreads, and draperies.

The consignment shop on the first floor sold homemade foods, including appetizers, dinner casseroles, cakes, pies, tea sandwiches, jellies and jams, breads, and fresh cinnamon buns. The merchandise shop sold fine collectibles, handmade quilts, baby clothes, and toys. Over the years, increasing costs, lack of parking, and competition from other stores made it too difficult to continue. The Women's Exchange closed its doors in 1996.

The Old York Road Garden Club was founded in 1935 by Mrs. Walter G. Thomson, Mrs. Robert Cridland, Mrs. Maurice Clair, Mrs. Thomas Montgomery, and Mrs. James Ray. At its peak in 1950, the club had a membership of 400. The garden club celebrated its 50th anniversary at a luncheon held at the Old York Road Country Club on November 14, 1985. Members are, from left to right, Nora Feeley, Bertie Wood, and Sandy Fritz.

The garden club's activities include workshops, tours, competing in Pennsylvania Horticultural Society events, and meeting at member's homes to see their gardens, as in this meeting in May 1997. From left to right are Hannah Warwick, Janice Levy, Sylvia Lin, Dorothy Leffler, and Burnis Witham. The club continues to meet monthly at Grace Presbyterian Church. Ongoing projects include the beautification of the Richard Wall House Museum in Elkins Park and the Jenkintown train station and outreach to schools and other youth groups.

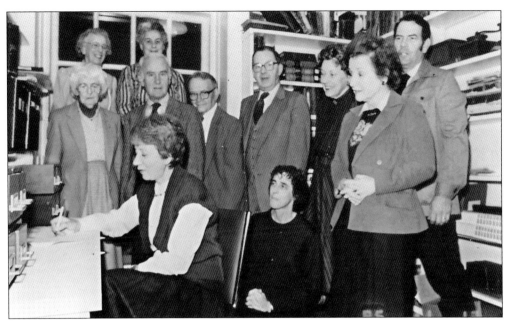

The Old York Road Historical Society was founded in 1936 with a mission to preserve and promote the history and folklore of the communities along and adjacent to the Old York Road. In the early years, three meetings were held annually, which expanded to five lectures a year. A scholarly journal, the *Old York Road Historical Society Bulletin*, has been published since 1937. In the 1980s, the society had an office on the second floor of the Jenkintown Library.

In 1992, space became available on the lower level of the library for an expanded historical society research facility. A ribbon cutting was held in the first-floor hallway in front of the doorway leading to the basement quarters. From left to right are state senator Stewart Greenleaf, society president Mary Ritchie, society archivist Francis Devlin, county commissioner Joseph Hoeffel, and state representative Charles Nahill. In 2012, the society relocated to Alverthorpe Manor.

The Old York Road Art Guild was organized in 1939 and presented exhibitions, art classes, and monthly talks. Many of the exhibitions, including the January 1956 show, were held at Strawbridge & Clothier's. In the early 1960s, the guild took up residence at the Abington Cultural Center (now Briar Bush Nature Center) and in 1970 relocated to Alverthorpe Manor, where it remains to this day. In 1978, the guild changed its name to the Abington Art Center.

The art guild held monthly presentations for the members, often meeting at the Strawbridge & Clothier store. In October 1956, local Pennsylvania Impressionist painter Arthur Meltzer (1893–1989) spoke. He was an artist who studied at the Pennsylvania Academy of the Fine Arts (PAFA) and was a longtime teacher at the Moore College of Art, where he served as chair of the fine arts department. He was married to fellow faculty member and accomplished artist Paulette Van Roekens (1895–1988).

Anna Heger, a young Irish immigrant, opened a dance studio around 1903 in a home built by her husband at the corner of Greenwood Avenue and Washington Lane. She started classes in the parlor, but a larger space was soon required, and so the old stable building was refurbished and enlarged for a proper studio. Her recitals eventually moved to the Jenkintown High School auditorium. By the mid-1960s, the school had closed. Many years later, the studio building was demolished.

The Curry School of Ballet was started by Shirley Curry in the basement of her home on Wyncote Road. This became her dance studio for many years. In 2010, Curry was presented flowers following the 50th anniversary show of her ballet school, which featured many of her former students. Her annual recitals were held in the Jenkintown High School Auditorium. (Shirley Curry.)

The Jenkintown Kiwanis Club hosted an inaugural dinner on May 12, 1949, where the club officers received their charter from the Kiwanis governor of the Pennsylvania District, Elmer Menges. For many years, the club met in the Methodist church at Summit Avenue and Walnut Street but recently moved to the Abington Friends Meeting campus. Previously a men's group, women were accepted as members starting in 1987.

From 1960 to 2001, the Kiwanis Club held an annual series of travel programs called Lecturama. The programs were held in area high school auditoriums, usually to sellout crowds. These events constituted the major fundraising activity for the club. At the ticket table are, from left to right, Kevin Corcoran, Ed Neale, and Lilian Flaherty selling tickets to Steve Cassidy and his son Steve Cassidy Jr.

In 1989, one of the community service projects of the Kiwanis Club was the purchase of benches along the SEPTA bus route 55 in Jenkintown and Abington. Shown from left to right are James N. Kirkner (Kiwanis president), Edwin Geissler (Jenkintown borough manager), Darrell Painter (executive director of the Jenkintown Chamber of Commerce and main street manager), Theodore Jensen (Jenkintown mayor), and John Tucker (SEPTA).

The main fundraiser of the Kiwanis Club since 1992 has been the Jenkintown 5K Sunset Run. Hundreds compete in this annual event as seen by the assembled crowds at Summit Avenue and Leedom Street in front of the former Salem Baptist Church. The run's proceeds are distributed to the many local charitable organizations that work with children and support the community. (Jenkintown Kiwanis Club.)

In 1954, the Jenkintown Music School, opened by Monroe Levin and Cameron McGraw, bought the Trumbauer-designed twin, the former Grace Presbyterian Church manse. After successfully operating for 15 years, an annex was opened in 1969 at the Abington Friends Lower School to accommodate additional students. In 1988, the school combined both facilities at Alverthorpe Manor. Shortly thereafter, the school merged with the Settlement Music School, becoming its Jenkintown Branch. In 2012, the school moved to its own building in Willow Grove.

Cameron McGraw and Monroe Levin were both pianists and met in graduate school at Cornell University. They came to Jenkintown and became codirectors of the Jenkintown Music School. McGraw (pictured at left with a student) was a composer of numerous works for piano, orchestra, and chorus. Levin published several books. They were known for their performances: duets (four hands) on both one piano and two pianos.

Seven

CIVIC AND SOCIAL

The Jenkintown Tigers of 1920 was an all-black baseball team. The team was active from at least 1917 to 1920 and played against other all-black teams in the various Negro leagues that were active at the time. Surnames of the players in 1917 include Moss, Campbell, Neuton, Tucker, Parker, Foreman, Gravey, and Moore.

On May 2, 1896, the annual Holbrook Road Race, organized by its promoter Joseph Holbrook, came to Jenkintown. Virtually all of the Delaware Valley bicycling clubs were represented. The 10-mile triangular course ran to Fox Chase and back. There were both amateur and professional races with cash prizes awarded to the winners. It was estimated that over 10,000 people watched the event. The above view looks south on Old York Road at West Avenue with a portion of the Cottman House hotel on the left. The view below looks across Old York Road to Greenwood Avenue. The rear portion of the Nice Brothers undertaking establishment is to the left and on the opposite corner is the home of Charles Wilson. Bicycle riding and races were very popular activities during the 1890s.

Begun in 1924 as the Women's Auxiliary of the Old York Road Hills Civic Association, the group was renamed in 1930 as the Woman's Club of Jenkintown. Its May 1932 meeting was held at the home of club president Elsie Smith Pollock at 510 Cheltena Avenue. Club officers are, from left to right, (first row) Mrs. Raymond Reinhart, Mrs. Harry Fritsch, Mrs. Schuyler Eves, Mrs. Benjamin Pollock, Mrs. Reginald Small, and Mrs. Harry Bird; (second row) Mrs. A.M. Redding, Mrs. David Scott, Mrs. Karl Lipp, Mrs. Charles Harvey, Mrs. Herbert Gledhill, and Mrs. Clarence Hambleton.

The Old York Road Contemporary Club was organized in 1934 by women who broke away from the Woman's Club in order to study current events and world affairs. They also hosted fundraisers to benefit the Willow Grove Air Base and the Valley Forge Army Hospital. In 1989, its members celebrated the organization's 55th anniversary. Cutting the cake are, from left to right, Edna B. Roman (president), Louise (Curry) Wakefield (mother of former state representative Lawrence Curry), and Marian Garrison. The club dissolved in 1992.

In 1913, the 1873 Masonic Temple building was heavily altered, and a new facade was added due to the generosity of brother Mason John Wanamaker. Until recently, the building was owned by Friendship Lodge No. 400, which merged into Concordia Lodge No. 67 in 2023. The building hosts many area Masonic lodges for their meetings. Also, the lodge hosts an annual open house following Jenkintown's Memorial Day parade when the public is invited to learn about the Masons, tour the building, and view a full-length portrait of John Wanamaker.

In 1967, Friendship Lodge celebrated its 100th anniversary. Twenty-five Past Masters came together for the occasion. From left to right are (first row) George Garrett, Leroy Ash, Abraham Clayton, Wallace Parrott, Harry Bloomer, and Harry Bracher; (second row) Joseph Rich, John Kerchner, Newman Lane, Albert Mathers, Herbert Gether, David Clark, and John McIntyre; (third row) Herbert Shoffstall, Raymond Humphreys, Ralph Hill, Edgar Plate, Clarence Martin, Edward Schoen, Walter Czarnecki, and Albert Raichle; (fourth row) Edwin Oberholtzer, Russell Schimpf, William Peterson, and Erwin Raichle. (Friendship Lodge No. 400.)

The Loyal Order of Moose is an international fraternal and service organization founded in 1888. Jenkintown's Lodge 1105 was founded in 1915 with a membership of 50. It originally met at the corner of Greenwood Avenue and Walnut Street where the MacSwiney Club is now located. The lodge moved to the 800 block of Greenwood Avenue in 1946 and later purchased 400 Cedar Street. They sold their building in 2003 and merged into Willow Grove Lodge 1101 based in Hatboro.

In 1970, the Scottish Rite Bodies of Freemasonry purchased the building on West Avenue below Runnymede Avenue that originally housed the carriages and stables for the Beechwood Inn. In the late 1920s, the building served as a suburban farmer's market; then became home to a company that made aluminum storm windows; then housed the Ferguson Manufacturing Company, which made roller conveyors; and finally was occupied by the Food Machinery Company. In 1984, the Scottish Rite sold the property, which was then demolished to make way for the One Jenkintown Station office building.

The MacSwiney Club was founded in 1920 as a branch of the Clan-na-Gael (Family of the Irish). It was an outgrowth of the Friends of Irish Freedom and has supported a free and united Ireland since its founding. The club was named for Terence MacSwiney, Lord Mayor of Cork, who died in an English prison on a hunger strike in 1920. The club met at various locations over the years, including 222 York Road (1933–1940) and 311 York Road (1940–1946). (MacSwiney Club.)

In 1946, the MacSwiney Club purchased 510 Greenwood Avenue as their clubhouse, the mortgage of which was paid off in 1949. The organization is private with few voting members but many social members. Since its founding, multiple generations of the Regan family have been involved in the club's leadership. Matt Regan Sr. was a longtime club manager until 2015.

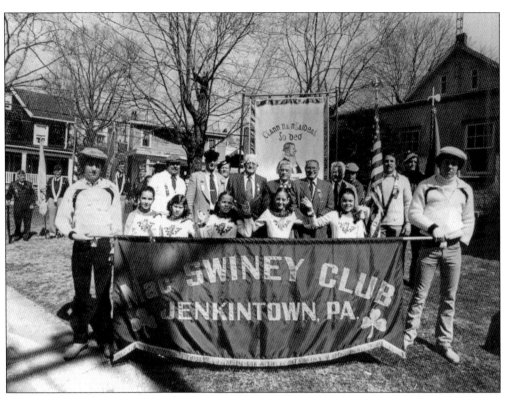

The club has actively participated in St. Patrick's Day events over the years, including marching in the main parade in Philadelphia. It presently celebrates "all things Irish," and there is traditional Irish dancing and music to help keep the culture alive and well. (MacSwiney Club.)

In late September 1994, Gerry Adams (right), the leader of Sinn Fein, the political wing of the Irish Republican Army, paid a visit to the MacSwiney Club as part of a 10-day tour to America. The visit was tacit acknowledgment of the significance the club's staunch support for Republican efforts has been. At the club, he viewed some of the many historical items in the club's archives. Adams stands beside John McPhillips, the longtime head of the Clan-na-Gael in Philadelphia. (MacSwiney Club.)

The Jenkintown Improvement Association was founded in 1909 for the purpose of reviewing and supporting activities undertaken by the borough to improve the community. One of the primary goals was to ensure adequate snow clearing of streets and sidewalks. From early horse-powered shoveling to more modern equipment, the association took the lead in keeping the sidewalks cleared. It also advocated for the enlarged post office and other civic improvements and enhancements. The association operated until 1980.

Based upon a 1980 Venturi, Rauch, and Scott Brown planning study "A New Main Street for Jenkintown" and a 1985 "Comprehensive Plan for Jenkintown," the Jenkintown Urban Mobilization Program (JUMP) was formed as a nonprofit. Its goal was to provide support and assistance to revitalize the central business district through grants and a full-time Main Street manager. Stephen H. Silverman, a Jenkintown-based attorney and JUMP board president, presented grants on October 19, 1990.

The Jenkintown Community Alliance (JCA) was formed in 1999 to facilitate the needs and concerns of local businesses. The group managed the Business Improvement District (BID), which was a self-funding business revitalization program. A BID was approved in 2007 but was rejected in 2012 given a continued decline in business activity and 33 empty storefronts. Today, JCA continues to sponsor an annual arts festival that draws thousands to the area. (JCA.)

The JCA-sponsored arts festival began in 2002 as the Jazz and Brew Fest and has evolved over the years to include many artists and craftspeople as well as live music. However, for many decades, Jenkintown has had an annual arts festival. The Jenkintown Chamber of Commerce held an arts festival in 1972, and throughout the 1970s and 1980s, the Jenkintown Library hosted a Festival of the Arts.

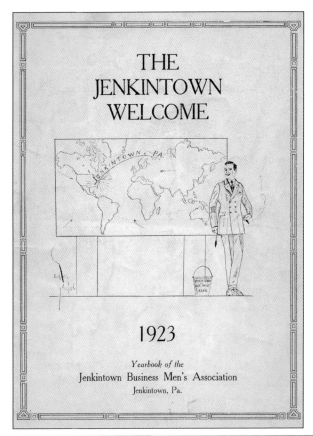

THE
JENKINTOWN
WELCOME

1923

Yearbook of the
Jenkintown Business Men's Association
Jenkintown, Pa.

The Jenkintown Business Men's Association was organized in 1918. Its 1923 yearbook recorded its events and members. In 1961, the association became the Jenkintown Chamber of Commerce and later the Greater Jenkintown Chamber of Commerce. By 1992, it again enlarged its geographical scope and became the Eastern Montgomery County Chamber of Commerce with offices on Old York Road in the former rectory of the Episcopal Church of Our Saviour. In 2022, it moved its offices to Fort Washington.

In March 1977, the Greater Jenkintown Chamber of Commerce held a St. Patrick's Day wine and cheese party at the Langman Gallery. In its efforts to promote local businesses, the chamber continues to host many informative, educational, and networking events for its membership.

In recent years, the Eastern Montgomery County Chamber of Commerce has held business expos, leadership seminars, and an annual awards dinner recognizing the best businesses, nonprofits, and volunteers in the area. At the 2009 Business Expo, staff, volunteers, and board members gather in front of the chamber's booth. From left to right are Wendy Klinghoffer (executive director), Jeanine Stewart, Stuart Tollen, Amy Chernow, Joanie Schnitzner, and Chris Heaven.

On January 18, 2022, then Pennsylvania first lady Frances Wolf came to Jenkintown to observe the National Day of Racial Healing. Local officials opened the event at the Jenkintown Town Square and then the group proceeded to a mural at 435 Johnson Street. Brian Bowens, artist (third row, far right), designed and painted the *Symbol of Solidarity* mural that was commissioned by Melinda and Stuart Tollen for the side of their building. Wolf is on the middle row, third from the right, and Melinda Tollen is next to her to the left. (Stuart Tollen.)

1874 == 1924

Jenkintown's Golden Jubilee

DECEMBER 1st to 8th

Here Are the Events:

MONDAY, DECEMBER 1st

Jenkintown Merchants begin distribution of coupons with every purchase. Make your purchases in Jenkintown AND SAVE THE COUPONS. Prizes will be awarded on Saturday Night, December 20th, to those holding coupons with numbers corresponding to the numbers on the prizes. Over $1000 in prizes are to be given away.
BUY IN JENKINTOWN

FRIDAY, DECEMBER 5th *12th*
GRAND PARADE

On Friday Evening at 7.30 o'clock, there will be a parade of the many organizations of the Borough—Floats, Bands, Automobiles. Lots of pep, gaiety and enthusiasm. Don't miss it.

SATURDAY, DECEMBER 6th *13th*

Football Game, between Jenkintown High School Team and Jenkintown H. S. Alumni
Aviation Stunts over Football Field by Flyers from Pitcairn Field
Hockey Game, Girls—Jenkintown H. S. vs. Abington H. S.

SUNDAY, DECEMBER 7th

A. M.—Special Anniversary Services in All Jenkintown Churches
8 P. M.—Union Services of ALL Jenkintown Churches in Auditorium of Jenkintown High School, 8 P. M.

MONDAY, DECEMBER 8th

Community Celebration of Jenkintown's Fiftieth Birthday and Granting of Borough Charter, 1874-1924. To be held in Jenkintown High School Auditorium.
Community Singing. Addresses by Prominent Speakers.

REMEMBER THE DATES AND EVENTS—DO YOUR PART

For Jenkintown's 50th anniversary as a borough in 1924, the community held a week of events from December 1 to December 8. Merchants gave out coupons to encourage sales. Special anniversary services were held in all the churches. There was a parade on December 5 and a football game the next day between the Jenkintown High School football team and the alumni. Aviation stunt flyers who came from Pitcairn Field in Horsham (today's Willow Grove Naval Air Base) also performed.

126

For Jenkintown's centennial anniversary in 1974, a banner was hung across Old York Road promoting the events held the week of September 20 to September 28. The festivities included a rocking chair marathon, ox roast, outdoor historical pageant with a cast of hundreds reenacting highlights of Jenkintown's history, exhibitions and displays, a centennial ball at Whitemarsh Valley Country Club, a pie-throwing contest, square dance, flea market, baseball games, and a carnival.

On the final day of the celebrations, a large parade was held with many floats and various organizations participating. The VFW Post 1711 color guard led off the parade followed by the post's Ladies Auxiliary and Colonial troop reenactors marching behind a fife and drum corps. In anticipation of the centennial events, Jenkintown men were encouraged to grow a beard with sideburns. While many of the whiskers were shaved off soon thereafter, a permanent record was published in booklet form that included many historical pictures and histories of Jenkintown and its various groups and organizations.

DISCOVER THOUSANDS OF LOCAL HISTORY BOOKS
FEATURING MILLIONS OF VINTAGE IMAGES

Arcadia Publishing, the leading local history publisher in the United States, is committed to making history accessible and meaningful through publishing books that celebrate and preserve the heritage of America's people and places.

Find more books like this at
www.arcadiapublishing.com

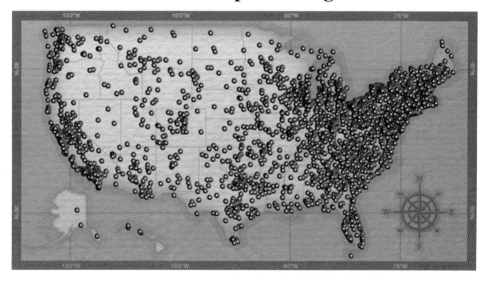

Search for your hometown history, your old stomping grounds, and even your favorite sports team.

Consistent with our mission to preserve history on a local level, this book was printed in South Carolina on American-made paper and manufactured entirely in the United States. Products carrying the accredited Forest Stewardship Council (FSC) label are printed on 100 percent FSC-certified paper.

MADE IN THE USA